piano | vocal | guitar

CANADIAN
ROCK & POP HITS

ISBN 978-1-4803-4165-4

HAL•LEONARD®
CORPORATION

7777 W. BLUEMOUND RD. P.O. BOX 13819 MILWAUKEE, WI 53213

For all works contained herein:
Unauthorized copying, arranging, adapting, recording, Internet posting, public performance,
or other distribution of the printed music in this publication is an infringement of copyright.
Infringers are liable under the law.

Visit Hal Leonard Online at
www.halleonard.com

ANGEL

Words and Music by
SARAH McLACHLAN

* *Recorded a half step higher.*

Copyright © 1997 Sony/ATV Music Publishing LLC and Tyde Music
All Rights Administered by Sony/ATV Music Publishing LLC, 8 Music Square West, Nashville, TN 37203
International Copyright Secured   All Rights Reserved

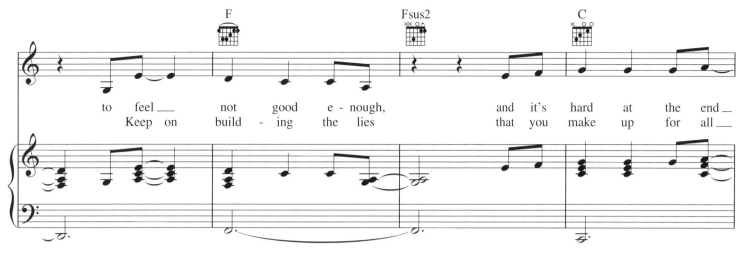

to feel ___ not good e - nough, and it's hard at the end ___
Keep on build - ing the lies that you make up for all ___

___ of the day. _____ I need some dis - trac - tion,
___ that you lack. _____ It don't make no dif - f'rence

oh, _____ beau - ti - ful re - lease. ___ Mem - o - ry
es - cap - ing one last time. _____ It's eas - i - er

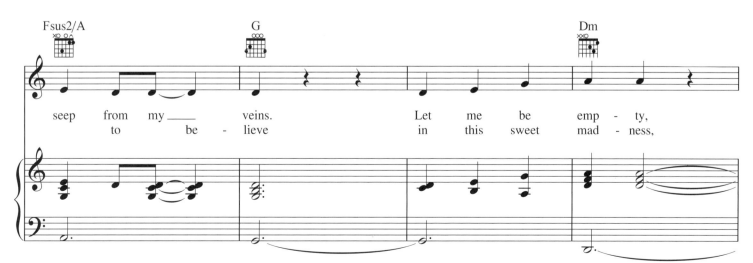

seep from my ___ veins. Let me be emp - ty,
to be - lieve in this sweet mad - ness,

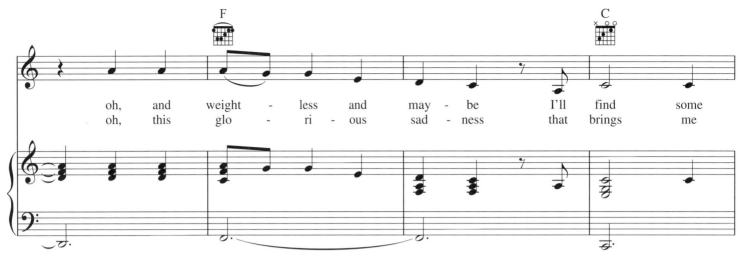

oh, and weight - less and may - be I'll find some
oh, this glo - ri - ous sad - ness that brings me

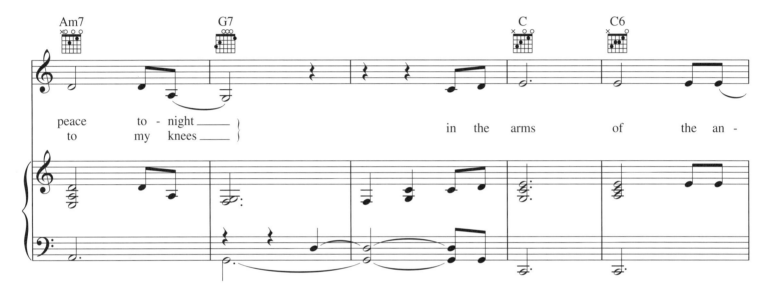

peace to - night _____ in the arms of the an -
to my knees _____

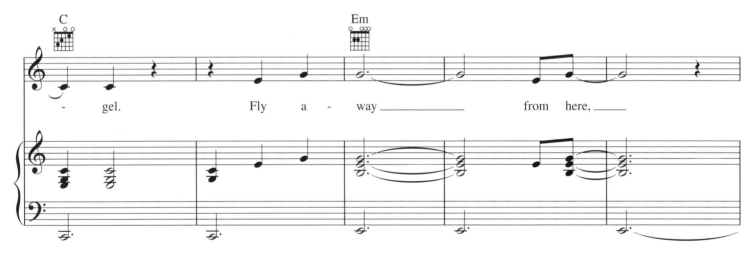

- gel. Fly a - way _____ from here, _____

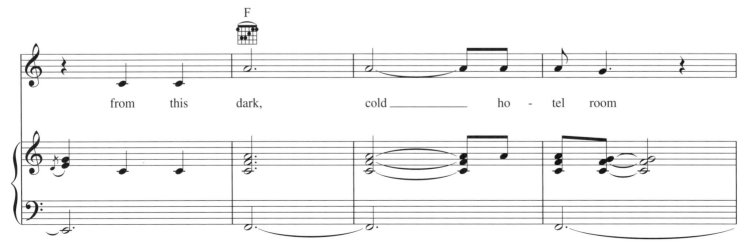

from this dark, cold _____ ho - tel room

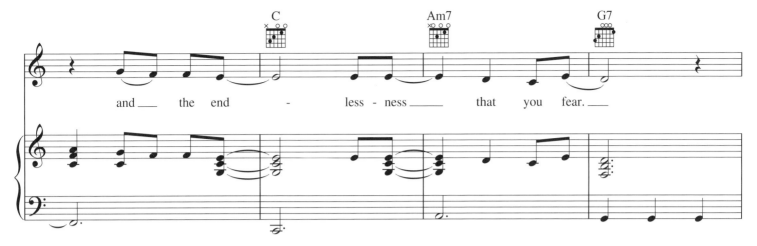

and ___ the end - less - ness ____ that you fear. ___

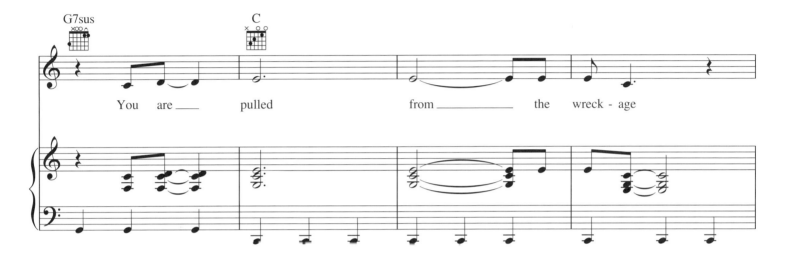

You are ___ pulled from _____ the wreck - age

of your si - lent _____ rev - er - ie. ___

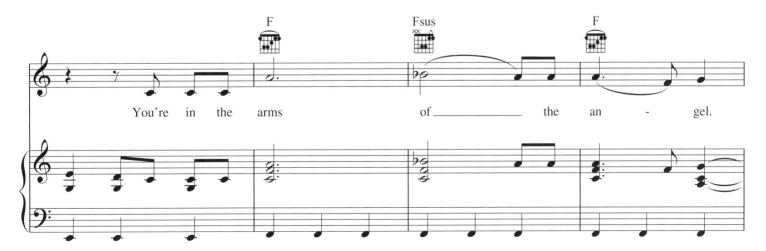

You're in the arms of _____ the an - gel.

To Coda

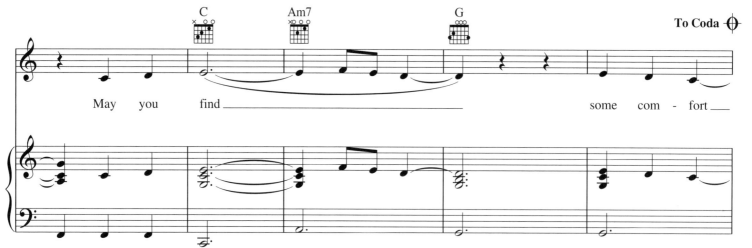

May you find _____ some com - fort _____

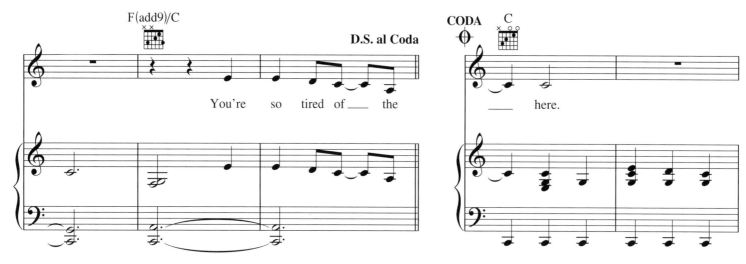

_____ here.

F(add9)/C

D.S. al Coda

CODA

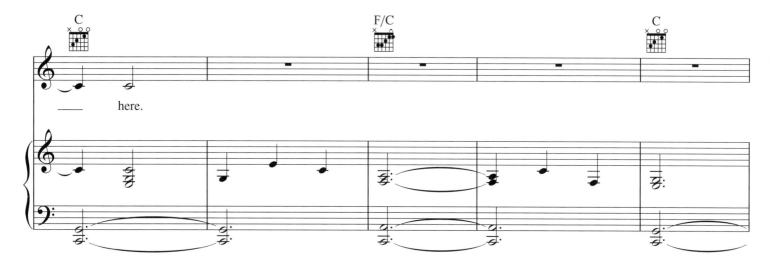

You're so tired of ___ the

_____ here.

You're in the arms of _____ the

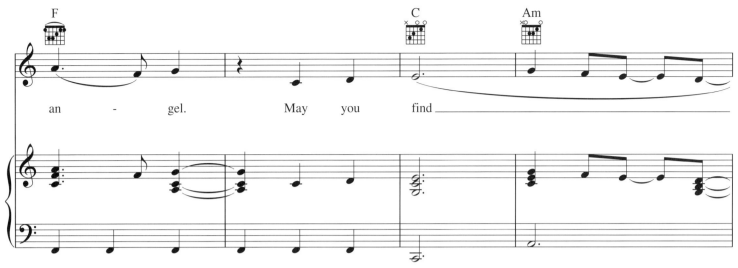

an - gel. May you find _____

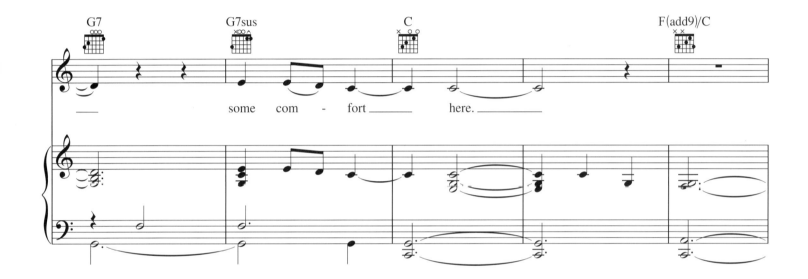

some com - fort _____ here. _____

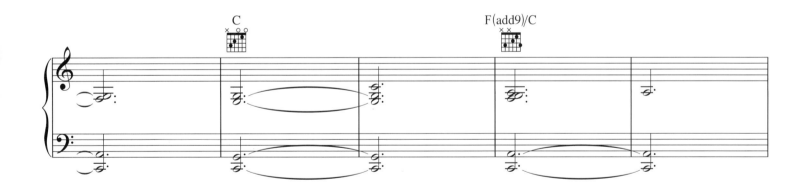

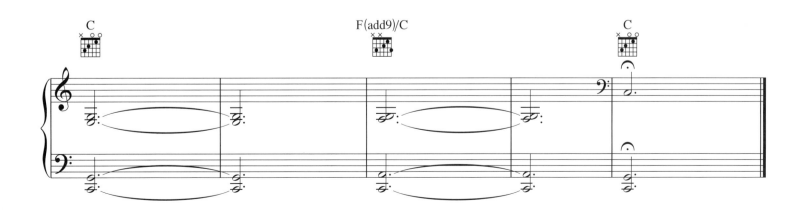

BOYFRIEND

Words and Music by JUSTIN BIEBER,
MAT MUSTO, MIKE POSNER
and MASON LEVY

Copyright © 2012 UNIVERSAL MUSIC CORP., BIEBER TIME PUBLISHING, SONGS OF UNIVERSAL, INC., MAT MUSTO, SONY/ATV MUSIC PUBLISHING LLC,
NORTH GREENWAY PRODUCTIONS, ARTIST PUBLISHING GROUP WEST and MASON LEVY PRODUCTIONS
All Rights for BIEBER TIME PUBLISHING Controlled and Administered by UNIVERSAL MUSIC CORP.
All Rights for MAT MUSTO Controlled and Administered by SONGS OF UNIVERSAL, INC.
All Rights for SONY/ATV MUSIC PUBLISHING LLC and NORTH GREENWAY PRODUCTIONS Administered by SONY/ATV MUSIC PUBLISHING LLC, 8 Music Square West, Nashville, TN 37203
All Rights for ARTIST PUBLISHING GROUP WEST and MASON LEVY PRODUCTIONS Administered by WB MUSIC CORP.
All Rights Reserved   Used by Permission

know a-bout me but I know a-bout you so say hel-lo to fal-set-to in three, two, swag.

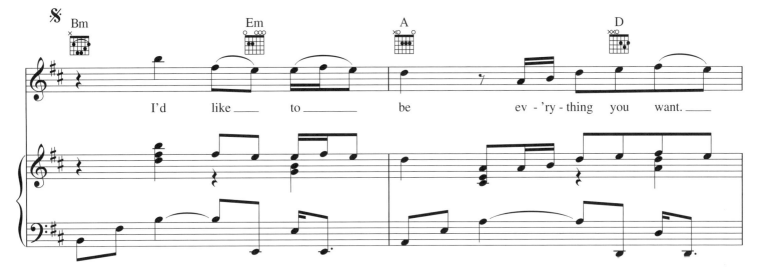

Bm   Em   A   D

I'd like ____ to _____ be ev-'ry-thing you want. ____

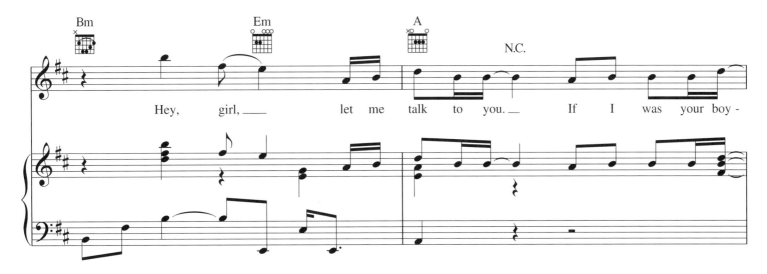

Bm   Em   A   N.C.

Hey, girl, ____ let me talk to you. __ If I was your boy -

Bm   Em   A   D

- friend, __ I'd nev-er let you go. ____ I'd keep you on my arm, __

girl, ___ you'd nev - er be a - lone. ___ And I could be a gen-

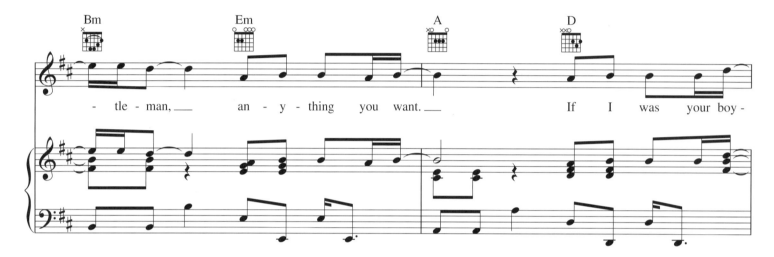

- tle - man, ___ an - y - thing you want. ___ If I was your boy-

To Coda

- friend, _ I'd nev - er let you go, ___ I'd nev - er let you go. _

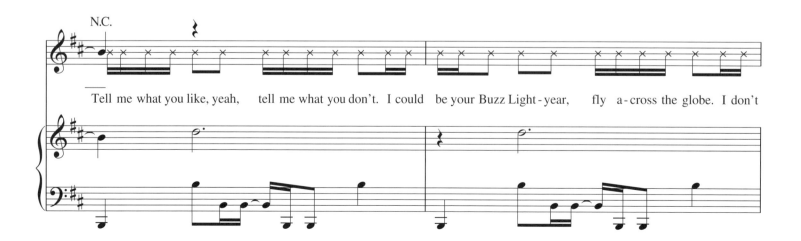

N.C.

Tell me what you like, yeah, tell me what you don't. I could be your Buzz Light - year, fly a - cross the globe. I don't

'cause you're all I need, _____ girl. ___ Spend a

week wit' your boy, I'll be call-in' you my girl-friend. If I was your man, __

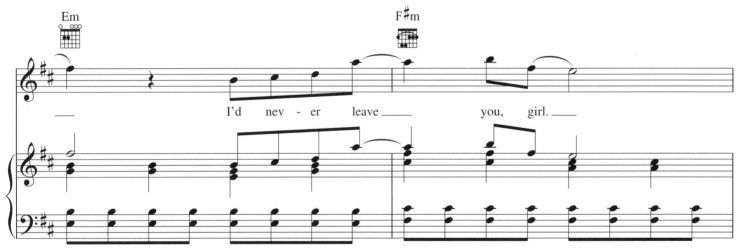

I'd nev - er leave _____ you, girl. ___

I just wan-na love and treat you right.
If I was your boy - friend, __ I'd nev - er let you go. __

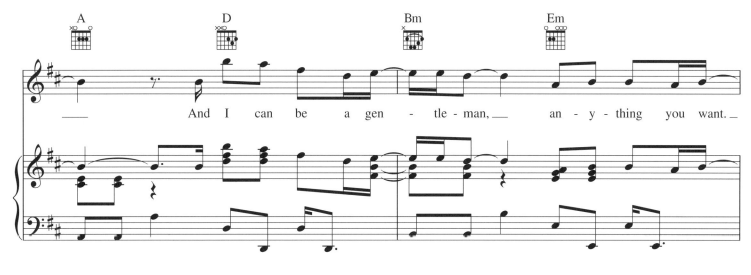

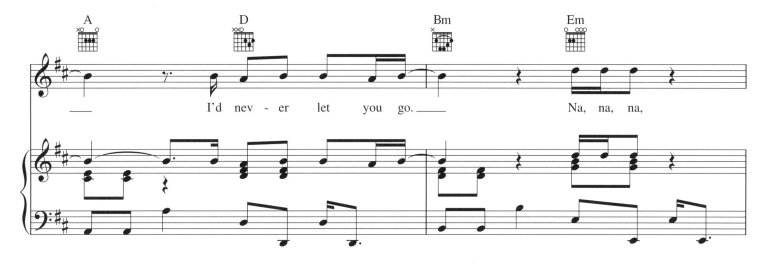

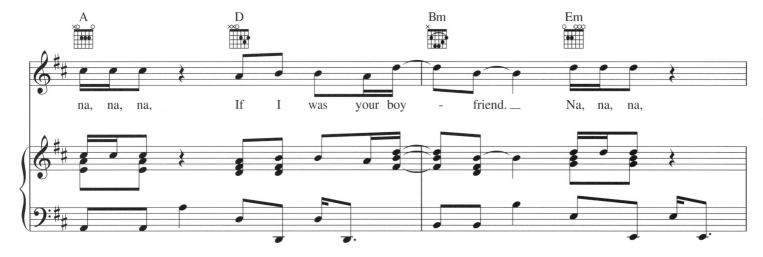

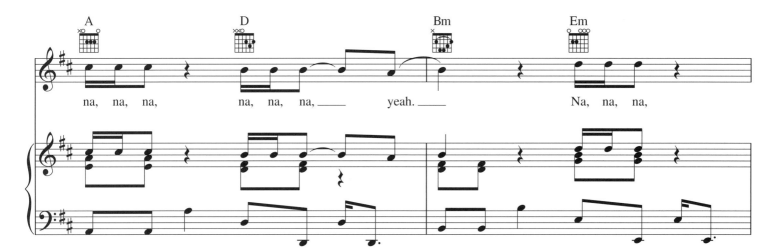

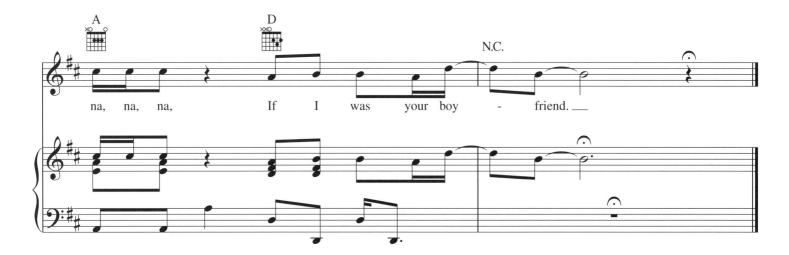

GRACE, TOO

Words and Music by ROBERT BAKER,
GORDON SINCLAIR, JOHN FAY,
PAUL LANGLOIS and GORDON DOWNIE

Moderately slow

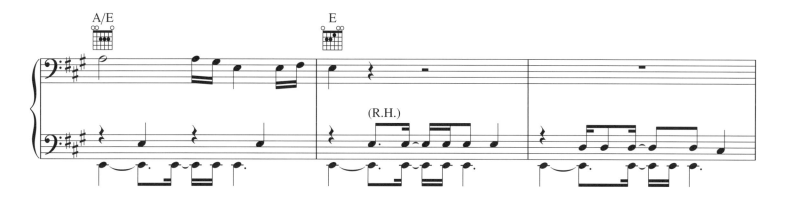

He said, "I'm fab - 'lous - ly rich.

Copyright © 1995 by Peermusic Canada Ltd. and Little Smoke Music
International Copyright Secured   All Rights Reserved

Come on, just let's go."

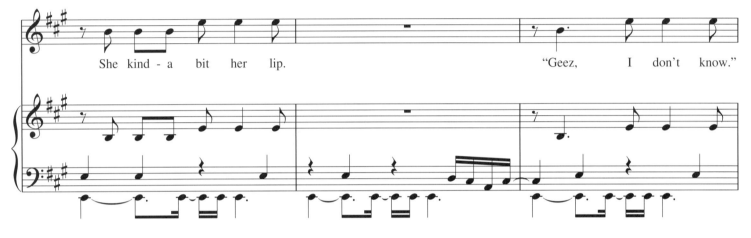

She kind-a bit her lip.   "Geez,   I   don't   know."

But I can guar-an-tee   (I can guar-an - tee)

there'll be no knock on the door.   (I can guar-an - tee.)   A to-tal   pro.

(There'll be no knock on the door.) That's what I'm here ____ for.

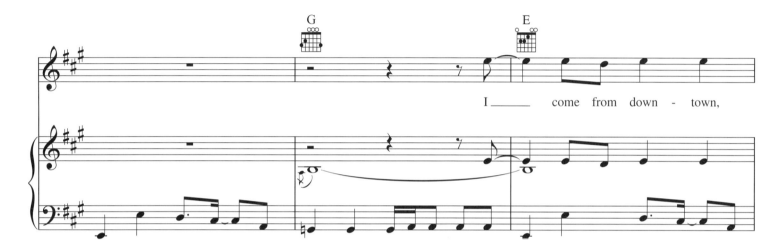

I ____ come from down - town,

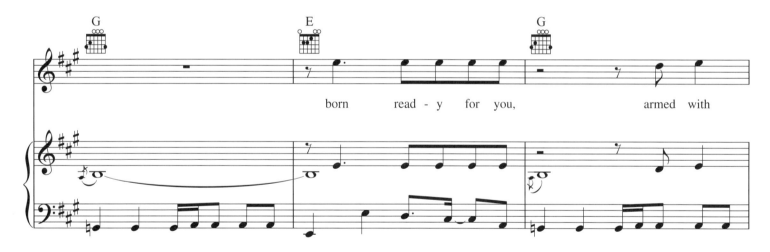

born read - y for you, armed with

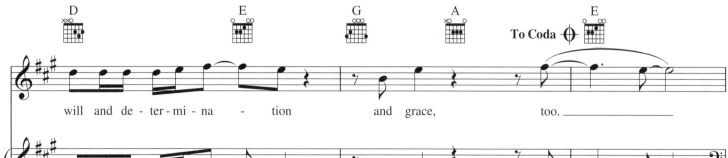

will and de - ter - mi - na - tion and grace, too. _____

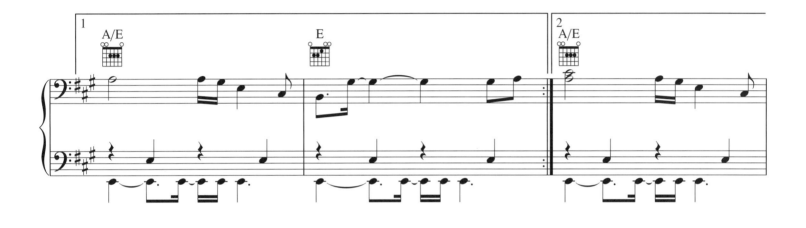

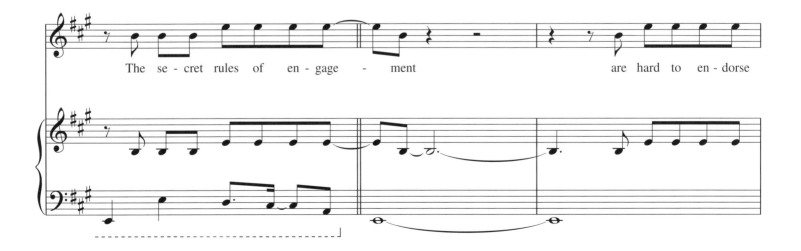

The se-cret rules of en-gage - ment are hard to en-dorse

when the ap - pear - ance of con - flict

D.S. al Coda

meets the ap - pear - ance of force.

But I can guar - an - tee

CODA

CALL ME MAYBE

Words and Music by CARLY RAE JEPSEN,
JOSHUA RAMSAY and TAVISH CROWE

Moderate Pop

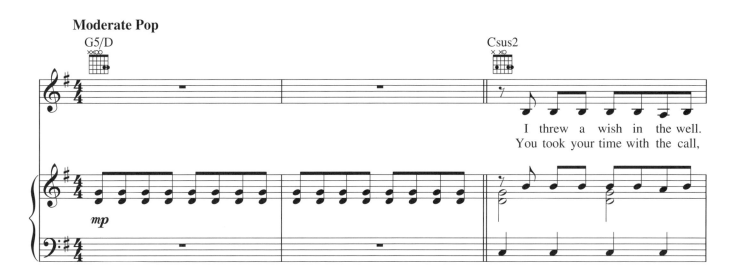

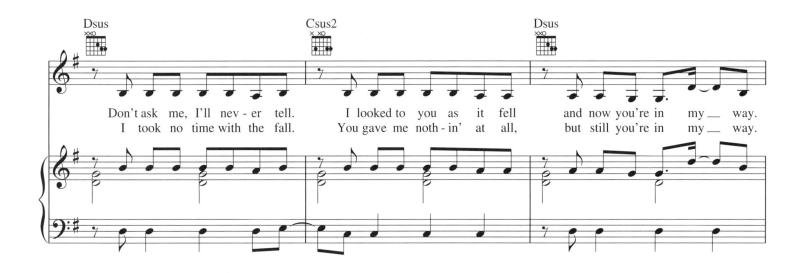

Copyright © 2011 UNIVERSAL MUSIC CORP., JEPSEN MUSIC PUBLISHING, BMG GOLD SONGS, CROWE MUSIC INC. and BMG PLATINUM SONGS
All Rights for JEPSEN MUSIC PUBLISHING Controlled and Administered by UNIVERSAL MUSIC CORP.
All Rights for BMG GOLD SONGS, CROWE MUSIC INC. and BMG PLATINUM SONGS Administered by BMG RIGHTS MANAGEMENT (US) LLC
All Rights Reserved   Used by Permission

but now you're in my __ way.
it, but it's in my __ way.
Your stare was hold - in'; ripped jeans, skin was show - in'.

Hot night, wind was blow - in'. Where you think you're go - in', ba - by? Hey, I just met __ you,

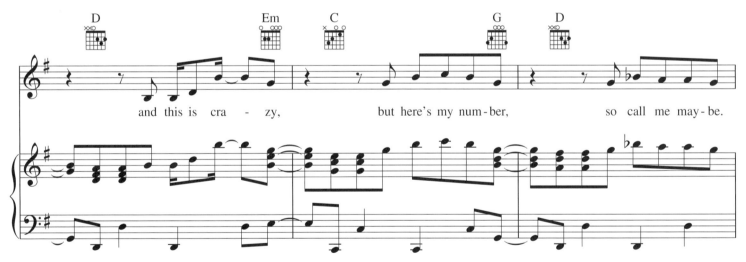

and this is cra - zy, but here's my num - ber, so call me may - be.

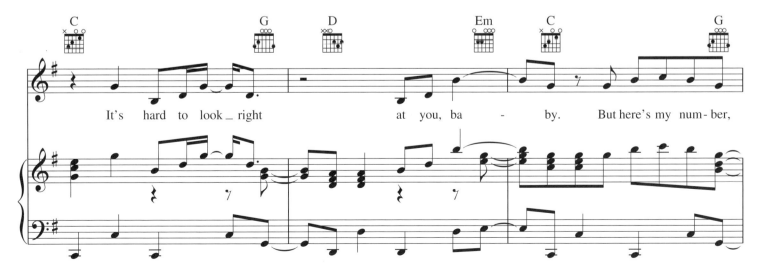

It's hard to look __ right at you, ba - by. But here's my num - ber,

so call me may-be. Hey, I just met __ you, and this is cra - zy,

but here's my num-ber, so call me may-be. And all the oth - er boys __

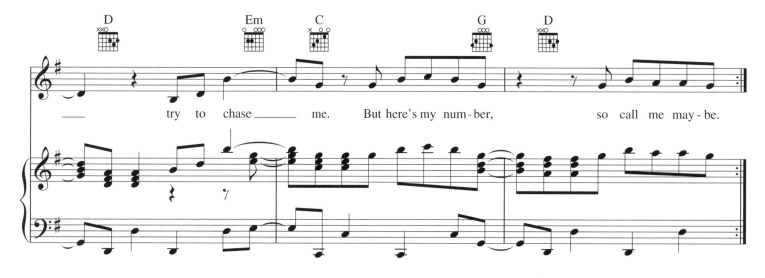

__ try to chase _____ me. But here's my num-ber, so call me may-be.

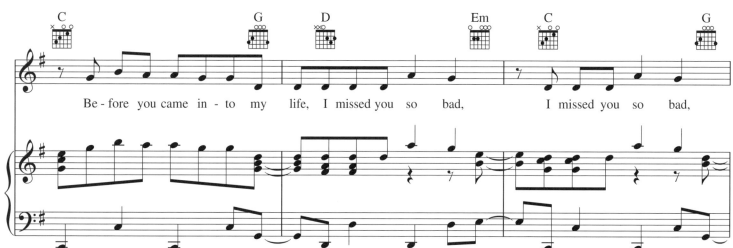

Be - fore you came in - to my life, I missed you so bad, I missed you so bad,

I missed you so, so bad. Be - fore you came in - to my life, I missed you so bad.

To Coda ⊕

And you should know that
And you should know that,

I missed you so, so bad.

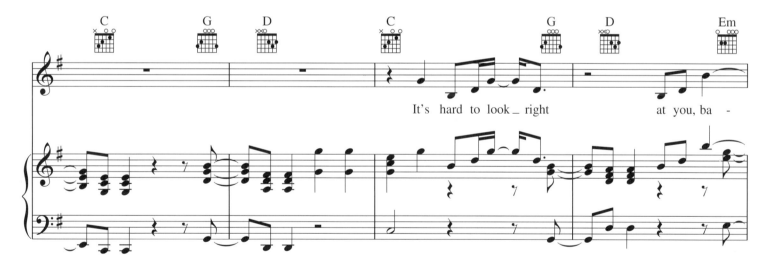

It's hard to look _ right at you, ba -

- by. But here's my num - ber, so call me may - be.

D.S. al Coda
(no repeat)

CODA ⊕

so call me may - be.

COMPLICATED

Words and Music by AVRIL LAVIGNE,
LAUREN CHRISTY, SCOTT SPOCK
and GRAHAM EDWARDS

Moderate Pop

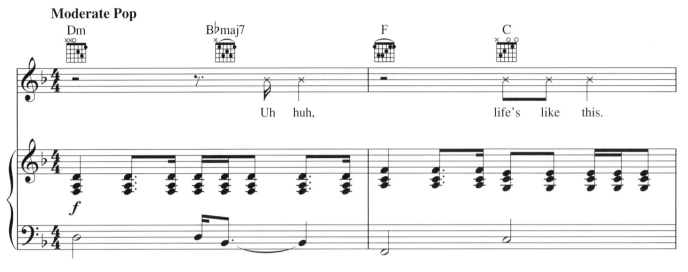

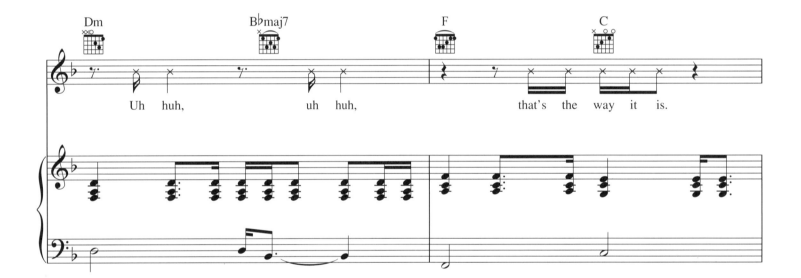

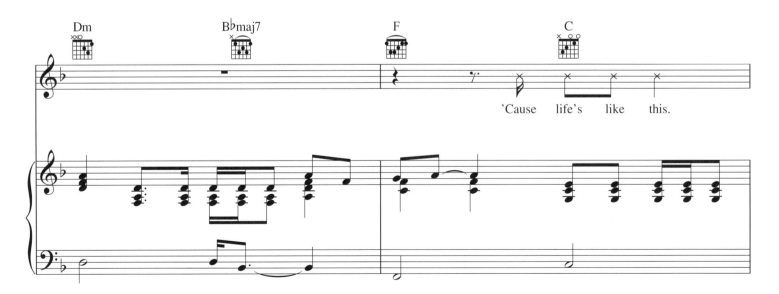

Copyright © 2002 ALMO MUSIC CORP., AVRIL LAVIGNE PUBLISHING LTD., WARNER-TAMERLANE PUBLISHING CORP.,
RAINBOW FISH PUBLISHING, MR. SPOCK MUSIC, WB MUSIC CORP. and FERRY HILL SONGS
All Rights for AVRIL LAVIGNE PUBLISHING LTD. Controlled and Administered by ALMO MUSIC CORP.
All Rights Reserved   Used by Permission

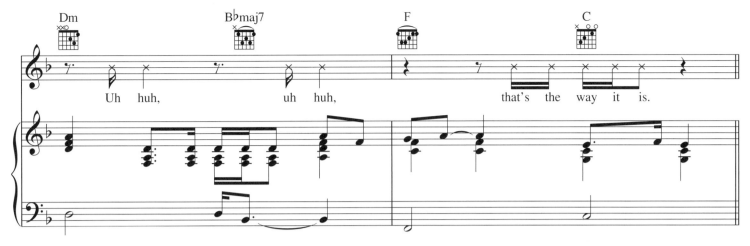

Uh huh, uh huh, that's the way it is.

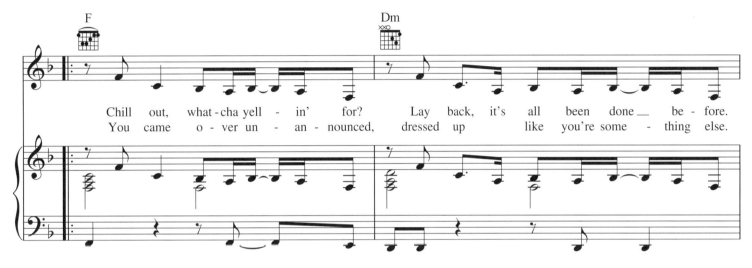

Chill out, what-cha yell - in' for? Lay back, it's all been done __ be - fore.
You came o - ver un - an - nounced, dressed up like you're some - thing else.

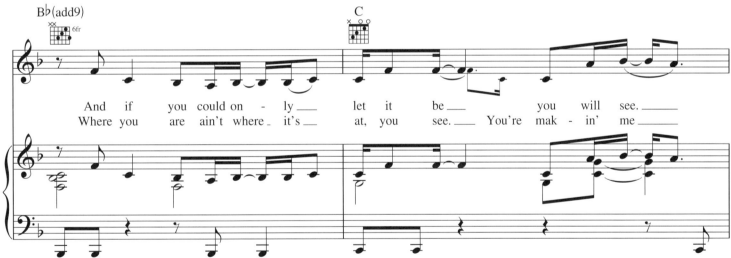

And if you could on - ly __ let it be __ you will see. __
Where you are ain't where __ it's __ at, you see. __ You're mak - in' me __

I like you the way __ you are when we're driv - in' in __ your car
laugh out when you strike __ your pose. Take off all your prep - py clothes.
Lay back, it's all been done __ be - fore.

and you're talk-in' to ____ me one on one ____ but you be-come ____
You know you're not fool-in' an-y-one ____ when you be-come ____
And if you could on-ly let it be ____ you will see ____

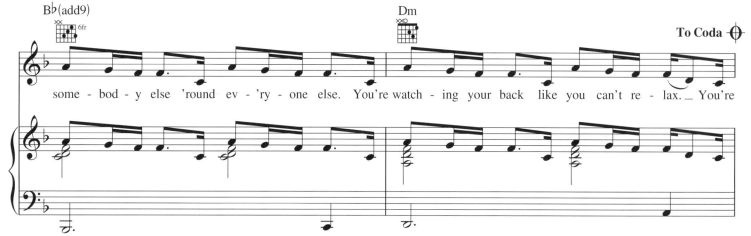

some-bod-y else 'round ev-'ry-one else. You're watch-ing your back like you can't re-lax. ____ You're

try'n' to be cool. You look like a fool to me. ____ Tell ____ me,

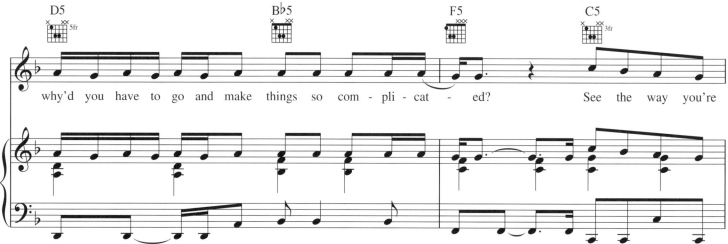

why'd you have to go and make things so com-pli-cat ___ ed? See the way you're

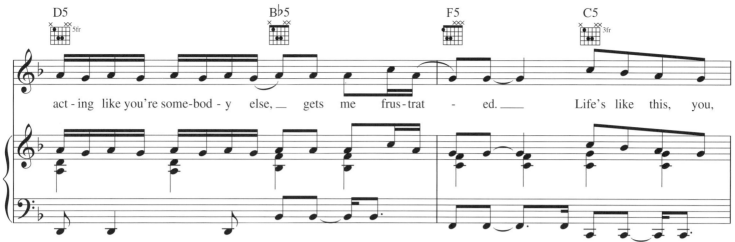

act-ing like you're some-bod-y else,__ gets me frus-trat - ed.__ Life's like this, you,

you fall __ and you crawl __ and you break __ and you take __ what you get __ and you turn __ it in - to

hon-es-ty and prom-ise me I'm nev - er gon - na find you fake __ it, ____ no, no,

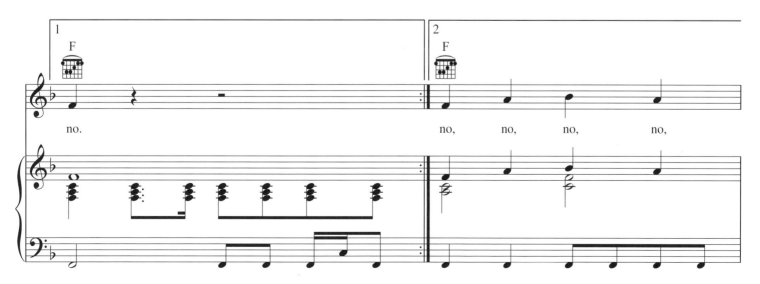

no.

no, no, no, no,

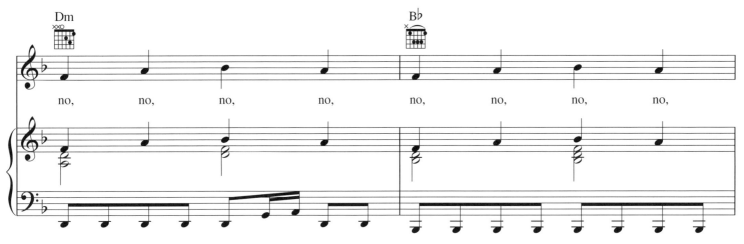

Dm   B♭

no,   no,   no,   no,   no,   no,   no,   no,

Csus   C   F   **D.S. al Coda**

no,   no,   no,   no. Chill out,   what-cha yell - in' for?

CODA   B♭(add9)   C5

try'n' to be cool. You look like a fool to me._____ Tell me _____

D5   B♭5   F5   C5

why'd you have to go and make things so com - pli - cat - ed?   See the way you're

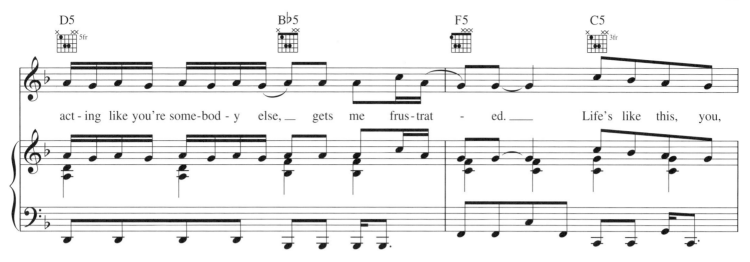

CONSTANT CRAVING

Words and Music by k.d. lang
and BEN MINK

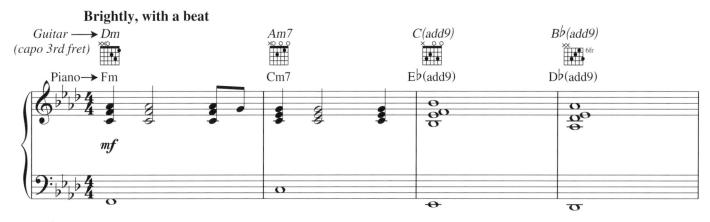

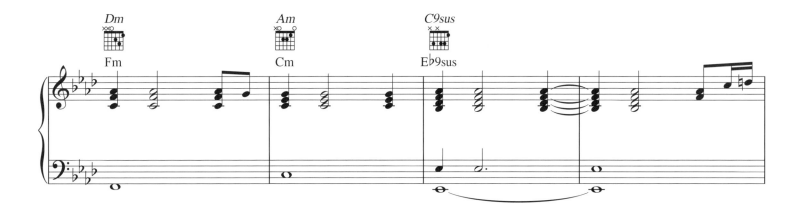

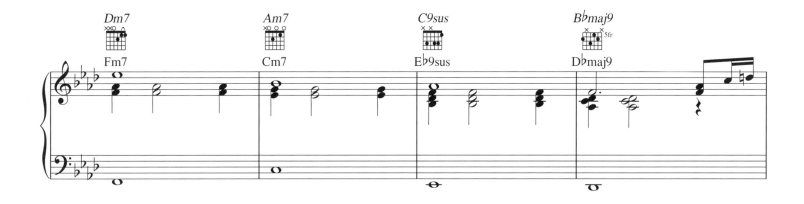

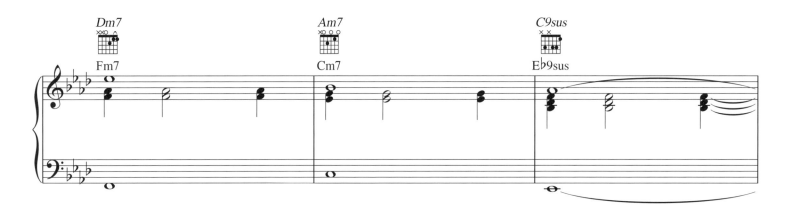

Copyright © 1992 UNIVERSAL - POLYGRAM INTERNATIONAL PUBLISHING, INC., BUMSTEAD PRODUCTIONS U.S., INC., ALMO MUSIC CORP. and ZAVION ENTERPRISES, INC.
All Rights for BUMSTEAD PRODUCTIONS U.S., INC. Controlled and Administered by UNIVERSAL – POLYGRAM INTERNATIONAL PUBLISHING, INC.
All Rights for ZAVION ENTERPRISES, INC. in the world outside the U.S. and Canada Controlled and Administered by ALMO MUSIC CORP.
All Rights Reserved   Used by Permission

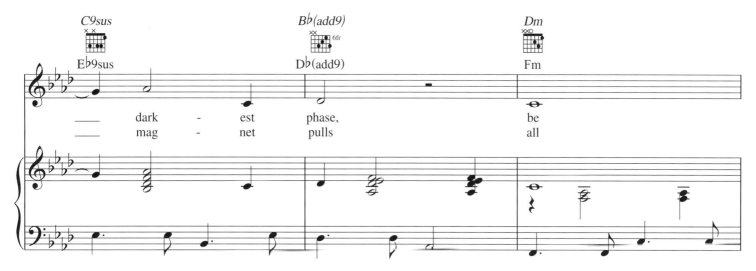

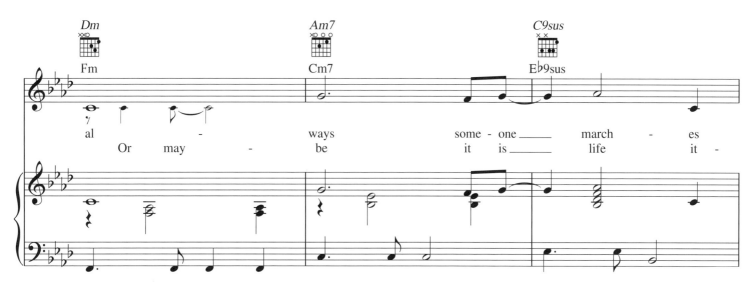

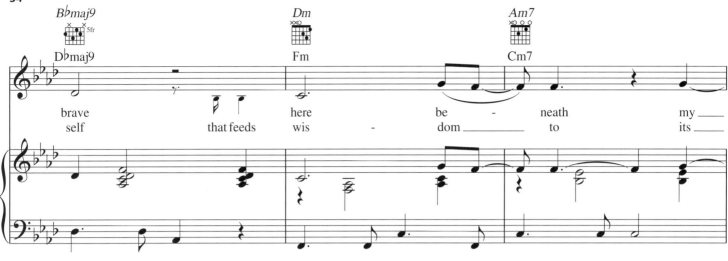

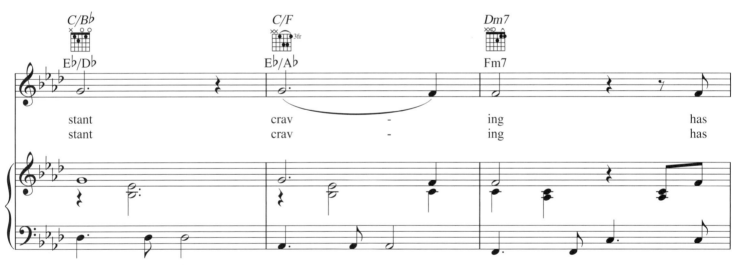

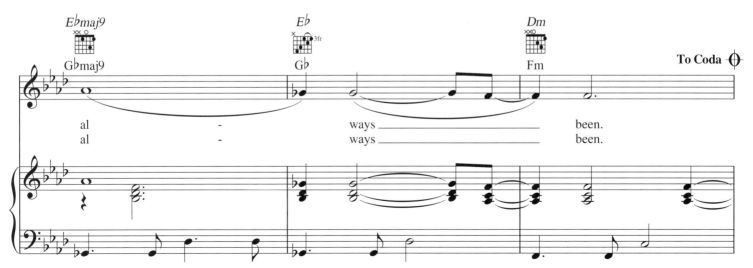

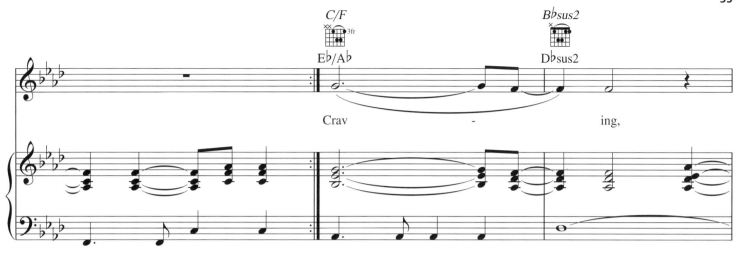

Crav - ing,

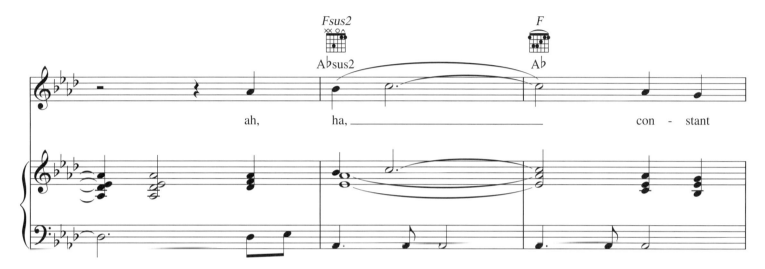

ah, ha, _____ con - stant

crav - ing has al -

- ways _____ been, _____ has

al - ways ___ been.

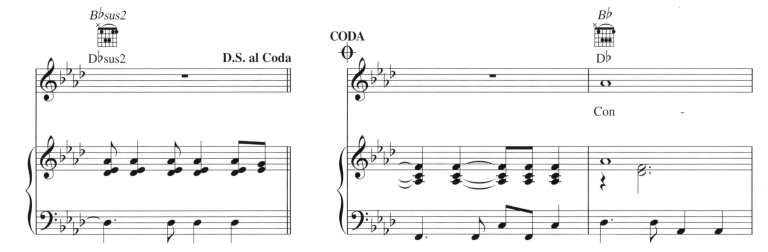

D.S. al Coda

CODA

Con -

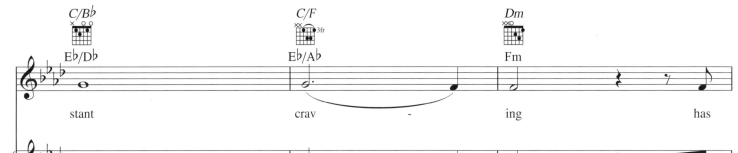

stant crav - ing has

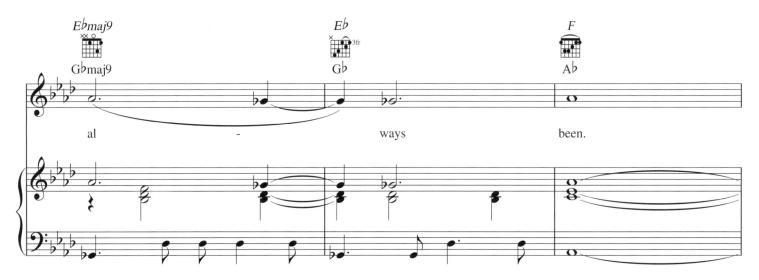

al - ways been.

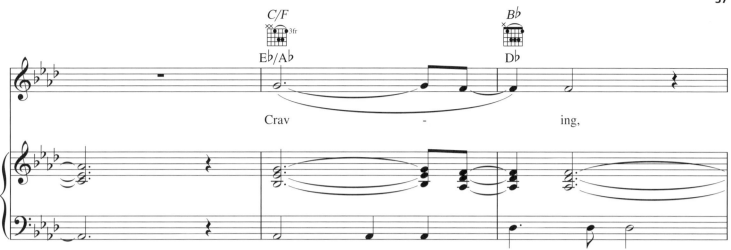

Crav - ing,

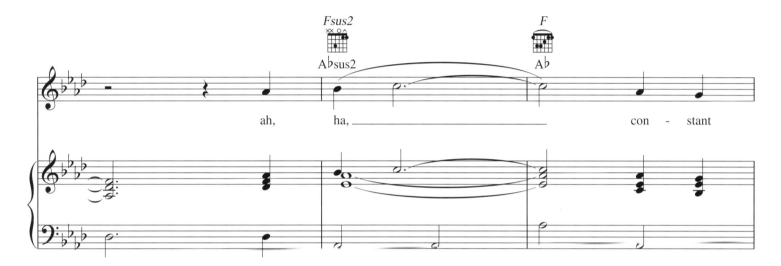

ah, ha, _____ con - stant

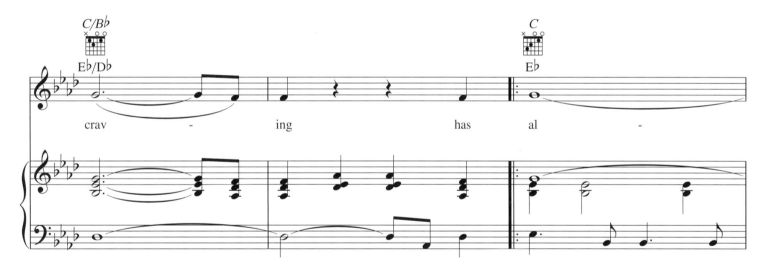

crav - ing has al -

Repeat and Fade

- ways _____ been. _____ Has

FAT LIP

Words and Music by
SUM 41

Storm - ing through the par - ty like my name is El Ni - ño, when I'm hang - ing out drink - ing in the
know us at all, we laugh when old peo - ple fall. But what would you ex - pect with a

© 2001 EMI APRIL MUSIC (CANADA) LTD., RECTUM RENOVATOR MUSIC, BONER CITY MUSIC INC., BUNK ROCK MUSIC, INC. and SHE GOES BROWN, INC.
All Rights for RECTUM RENOVATOR MUSIC in the U.S. Controlled and Administered by EMI APRIL MUSIC INC.
All Rights for BONER CITY MUSIC INC. Controlled and Administered by EMI APRIL MUSIC INC.
All Rights Reserved   International Copyright Secured   Used by Permission

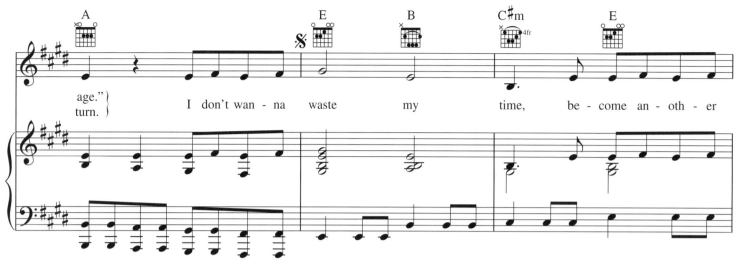

age."
turn.
I don't wan - na waste my time, be - come an - oth - er

cas - ual - ty of so - ci - e - ty. I'll nev - er fall in

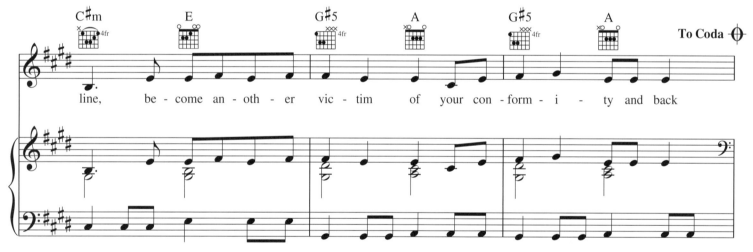

To Coda

line, be - come an - oth - er vic - tim of your con - form - i - ty and back

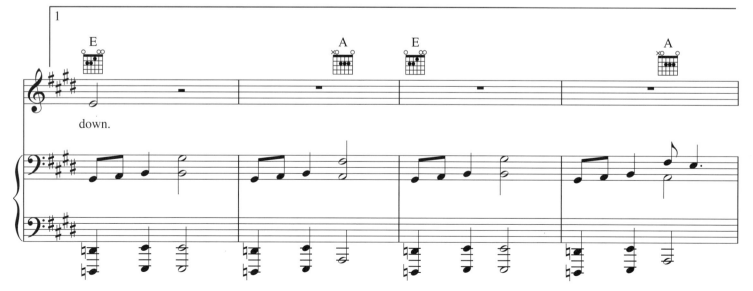

1

down.

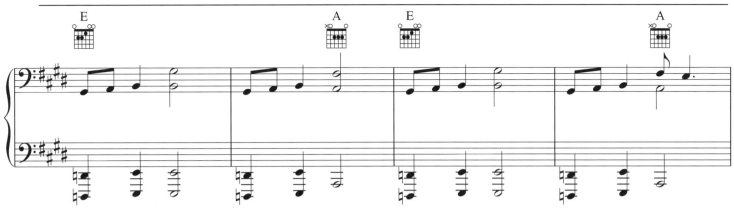

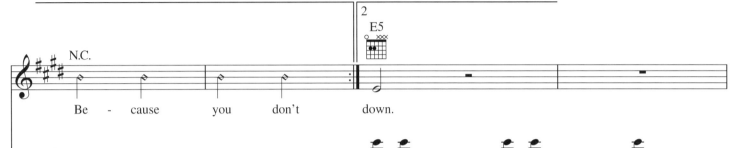

Be - cause you don't down.

Don't count on me ___

ci - e - ty.

Waste my time ____ with them. __

Vic - tim of your con - form - i - ty and back down.

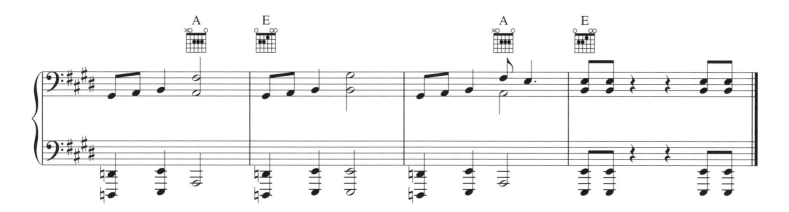

HAVE YOU EVER REALLY LOVED A WOMAN?

from the Motion Picture DON JUAN DeMARCO

Words and Music by BRYAN ADAMS,
MICHAEL KAMEN and R.J. LANGE

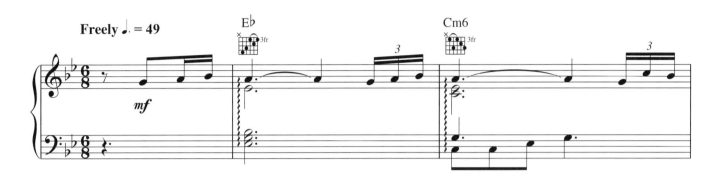

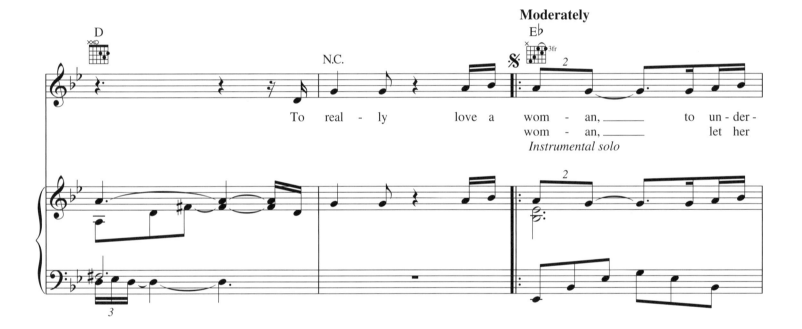

To real-ly love a wom-an, _____ to un-der-
wom-an, _____ let her
Instrumental solo

stand her, _____ you got-ta know her deep in-side; _____ hear ev-'ry
hold you, _____ till ya know how she needs to be touched. _ You've got-ta

© 1994, 1995 BADAMS MUSIC LTD., SONY/ATV MUSIC PUBLISHING LLC, NEW LINE MUSIC, K-MAN CORP. and UNIVERSAL MUSIC - Z TUNES LLC
All Rights on behalf of BADAMS MUSIC LTD. Administered by EMI APRIL MUSIC INC.
All Rights on behalf of SONY/ATV MUSIC PUBLISHING LLC, NEW LINE MUSIC and K-MAN CORP. Administered by SONY/ATV MUSIC PUBLISHING LLC, 8 Music Square West, Nashville, TN 37203
All Rights Reserved   International Copyright Secured   Used by Permission

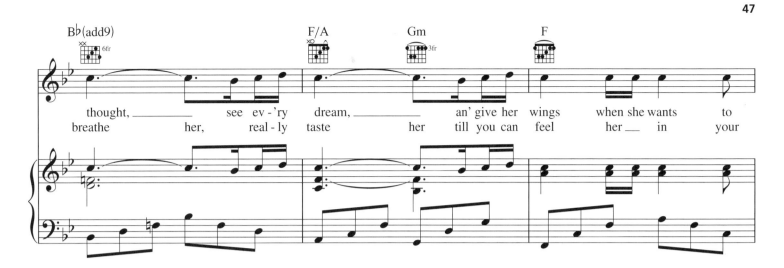

thought, _____ see ev -'ry dream, _____ an' give her wings when she wants to
breathe her, real - ly taste her till you can feel her ___ in your

fly. _____ Then when you find your-self ly - in' help 2 -less _____ in her
blood. ___ When you can see _____ your un - born chil - dren _____ in her
Solo ends Then when you find your-self ly - in' help - less _____ in her

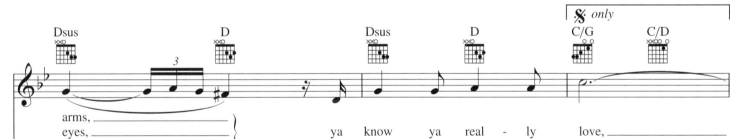

arms, _____
eyes, _____   ya know ya real - ly love, _____
arms, _____

% only

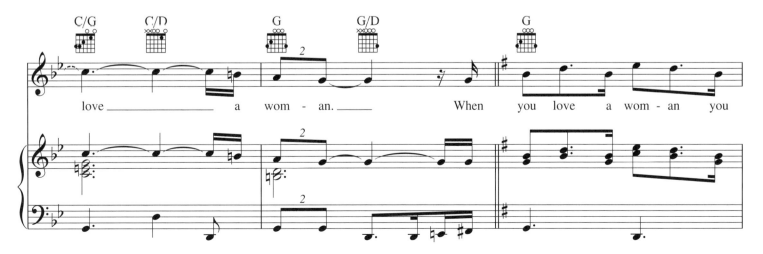

love _____ a wom - an. _____ When you love a wom - an you

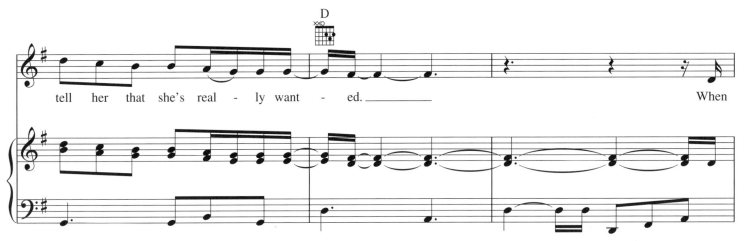

tell her that she's real - ly want - ed. _____ When

you love a wom - an you tell her that she's _____ the one, _____

'cause she needs some-bod - y to tell her that it's gon - na last _

'cause she needs some-bod - y to tell her that you'll al - ways be. _

_____ for - ev - er. _____

_____ to - geth - er. _____

So tell me have you ev - er real - ly,

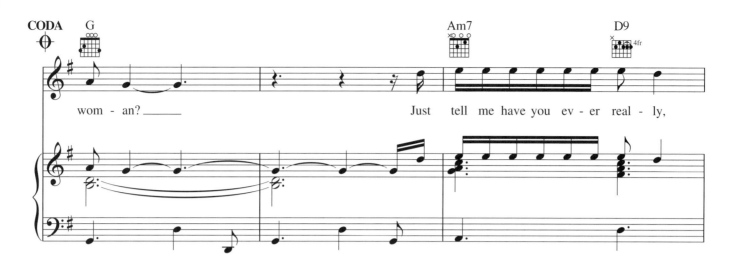

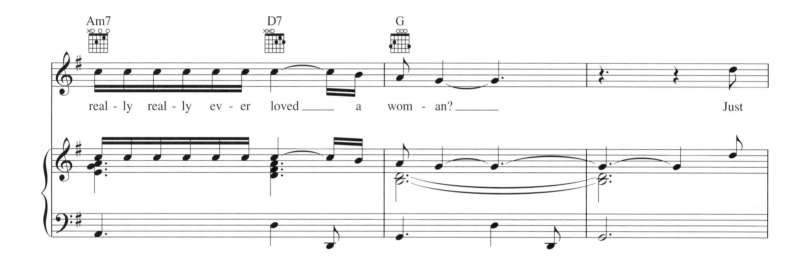

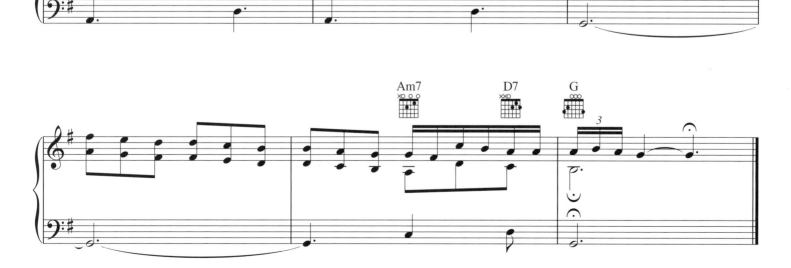

HALLELUJAH

Words and Music by
LEONARD COHEN

Copyright © 1995 Sony/ATV Music Publishing LLC
All Rights Administered by Sony/ATV Music Publishing LLC, 8 Music Square West, Nashville, TN 37203
International Copyright Secured   All Rights Reserved

HAVEN'T MET YOU YET

Words and Music by MICHAEL BUBLÉ,
ALAN CHANG and AMY FOSTER

* Recorded a half step higher.

© 2009 WB MUSIC CORP., I'M THE LAST MAN STANDING MUSIC, INC., WARNER-TAMERLANE PUBLISHING CORP., IHAN ZHAN MUSIC and MS. DOE MUSIC
All Rights for I'M THE LAST MAN STANDING MUSIC, INC. Administered by WB MUSIC CORP.
All Rights for IHAN ZHAN MUSIC and MS. DOE MUSIC Administered by WARNER-TAMERLANE PUBLISHING CORP.
All Rights Reserved   Used by Permission

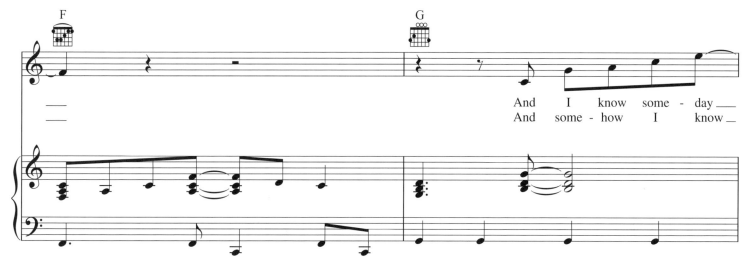

And I know some - day ___
And some - how I know ___

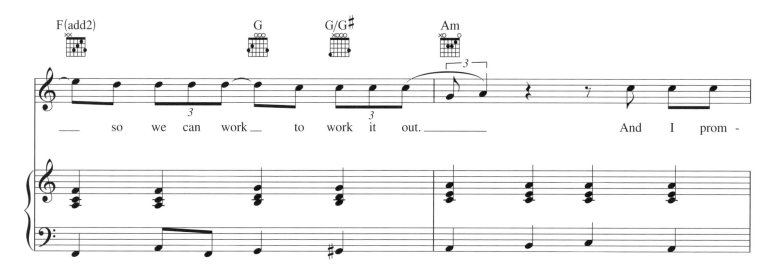

that it - 'll all ___ turn out; ___ you'll make me work ___

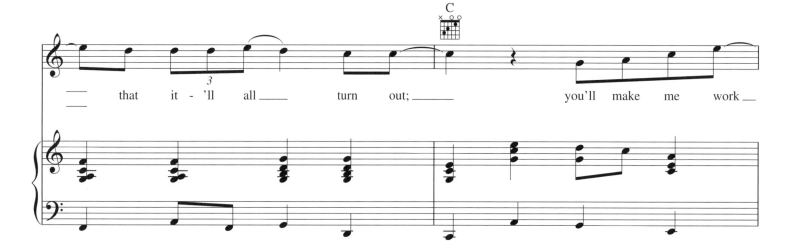

___ so we can work ___ to work it out. ___ And I prom -

ise you, kid, ___ that I'll give ___ so much more ___ than I get, ___ mm; I

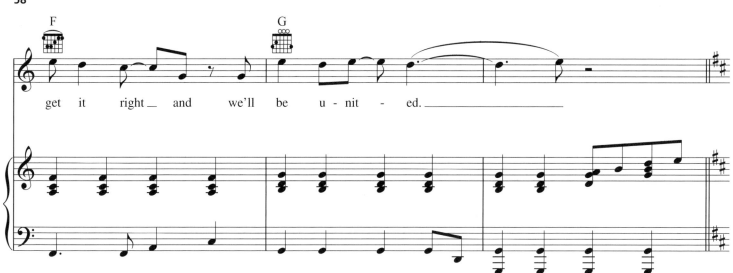

get it right __ and we'll be u - nit - ed. _____

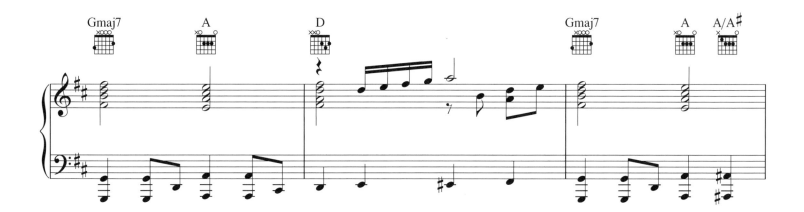

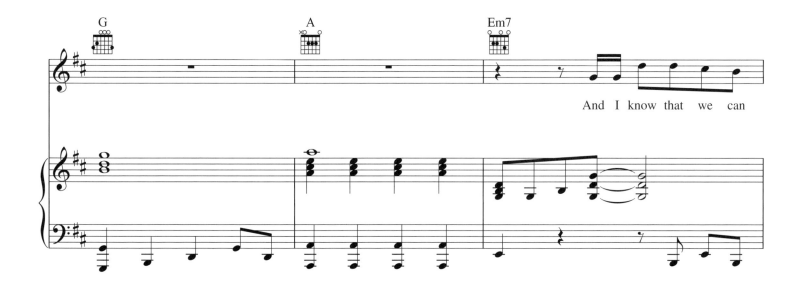

And I know that we can

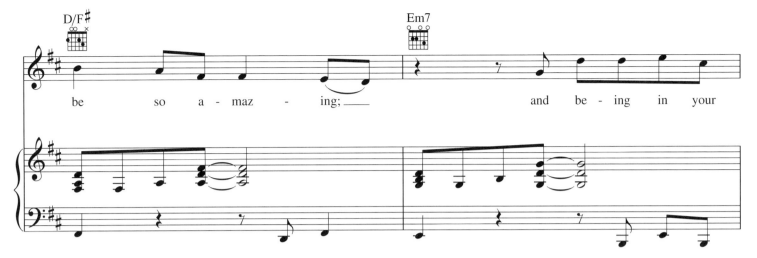

be so a-maz - ing; _____ and be-ing in your

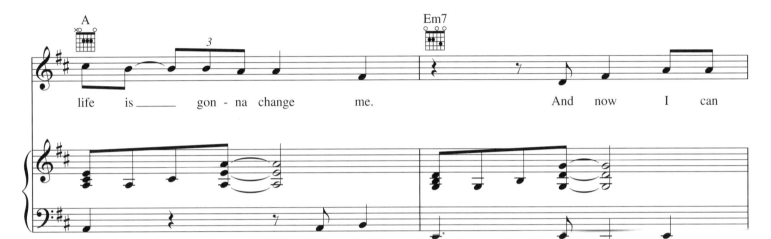

life is _____ gon-na change me. And now I can

see ev-'ry sin-gle pos - si-bil-i-ty, _____ mm. _____

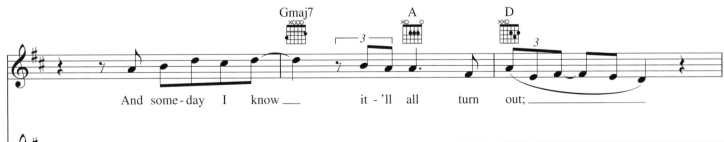

And some-day I know ___ it -'ll all turn out; _____

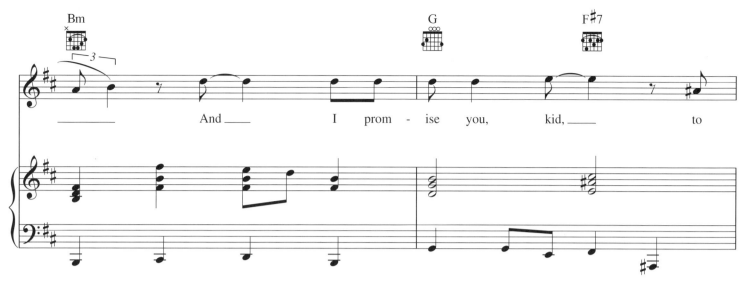

And ___ I prom - ise you, kid, ___ to

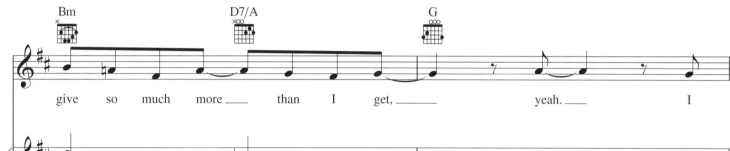

give so much more ___ than I get, ___ yeah. ___ I

just have - n't ___ met you yet.

I just have - n't met you yet. Oh,

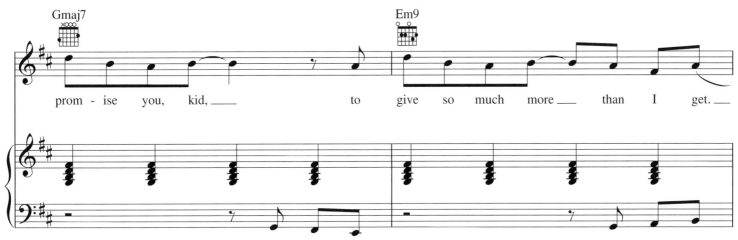

prom - ise you, kid, ___ to give so much more ___ than I get. ___

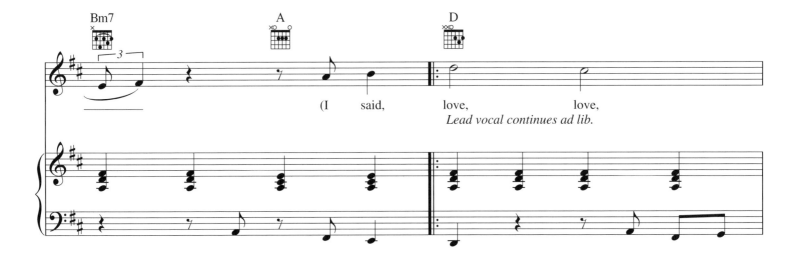

(I said, love, love,

Lead vocal continues ad lib.

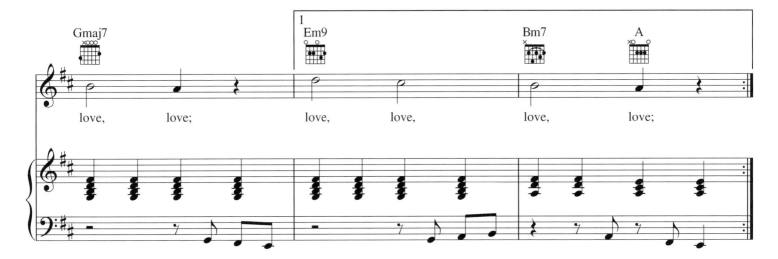

love, love; love, love, love, love;

love, love.) I just have - n't met you yet.

IT'S ALL COMING BACK TO ME NOW

Words and Music by
JIM STEINMAN

Copyright © 1989 UNIVERSAL - SONGS OF POLYGRAM INTERNATIONAL, INC. and LOST BOYS MUSIC
All Rights Controlled and Administered by UNIVERSAL - SONGS OF POLYGRAM INTERNATIONAL, INC.
All Rights Reserved   Used by Permission

touch me like this, ____ and you hold me like that, ____ I just
touch you like this, ____ and if you kiss me like that, ____ it was

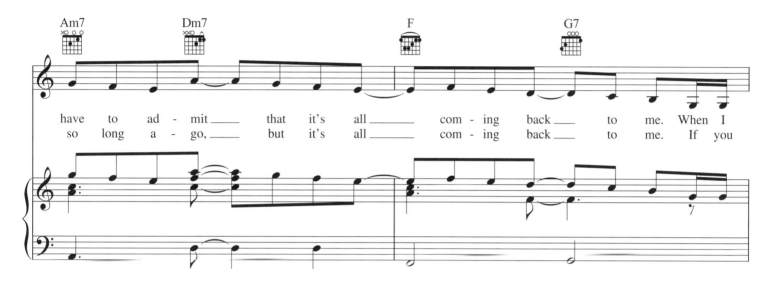

have to ad - mit ____ that it's all ____ com - ing back ____ to me. When I
so long a - go, ____ but it's all ____ com - ing back ____ to me. If you

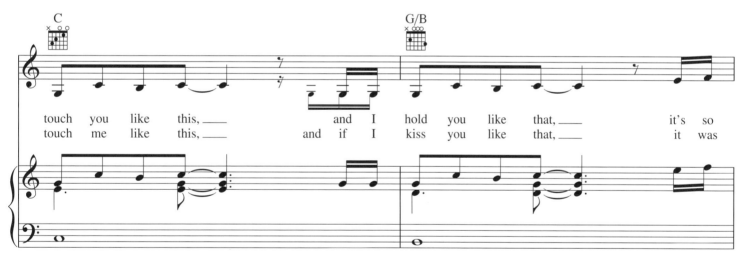

touch you like this, ____ and I hold you like that, ____ it's so
touch me like this, ____ and if I kiss you like that, ____ it was

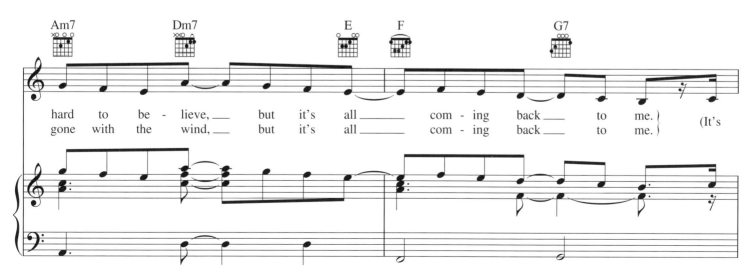

hard to be - lieve, ____ but it's all ____ com - ing back ____ to me. }
gone with the wind, ____ but it's all ____ com - ing back ____ to me. } (It's

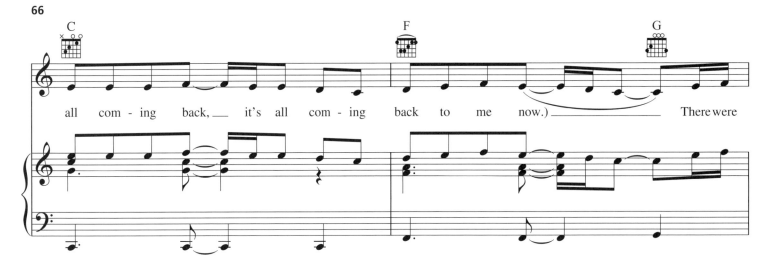

all com-ing back, ___ it's all com-ing back to me now.) _____ There were

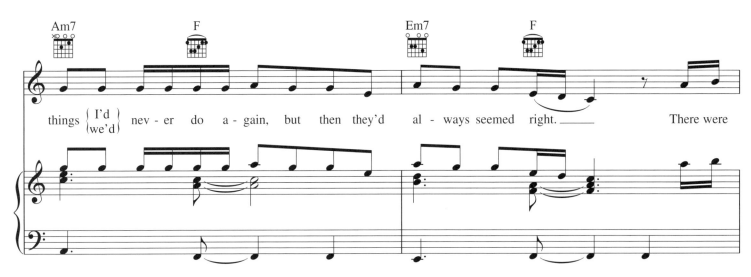

mo-ments of gold, ___ and there were flash-es of light. _____ There were

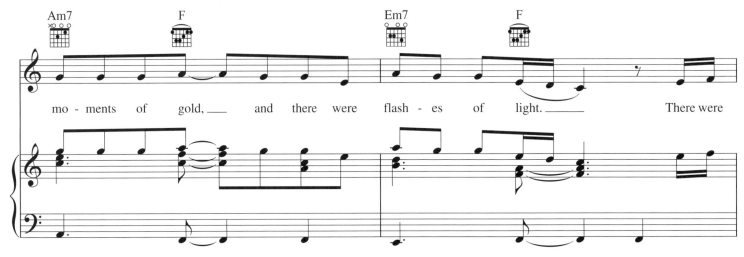

things {I'd / we'd} nev-er do a-gain, but then they'd al-ways seemed right. _____ There were

nights of end-less pleas-ure. It was more than {an-y / all your} lov-ers in love. _____

Baby, baby if I kiss you like this, _____ and if you
Ba - by, ba - by, ba - by, when you touch me like this, _____ and when you

rall.　*a tempo*

whis - per like that, _____ it was lost long a - go, _____ but it's all _____
hold me like that, _____ it was gone with the wind, _____ but it's all _____

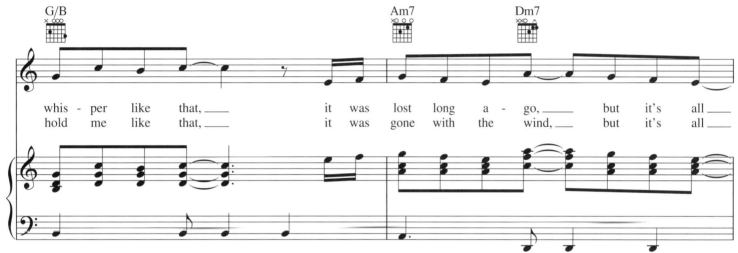

_____ com - ing back _____ to me. If you want me like this, _____ and if you
_____ com - ing back _____ to me. When you see me like this, _____ and when I

need me like that, _____ it was that long a - go, _____ but it's all _____
see you like that, _____ then we've seen what we want _____ to see, all _____

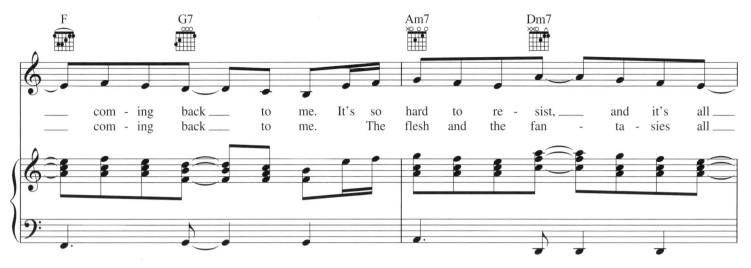

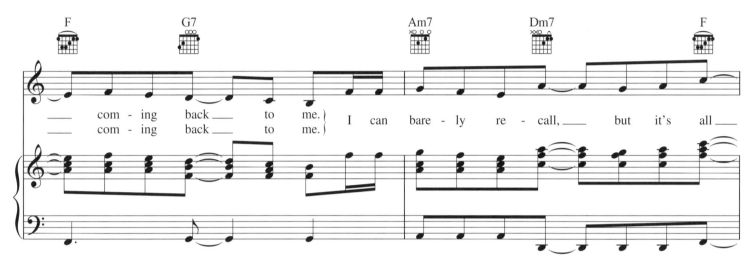

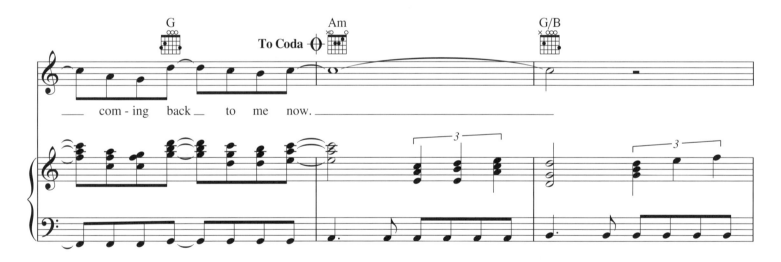

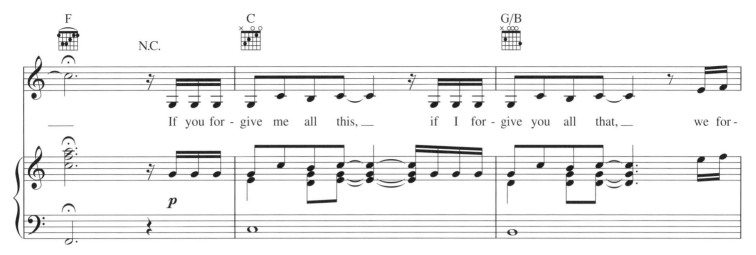

HOW YOU REMIND ME

Words by CHAD KROEGER
Music by NICKELBACK

Moderately slow

Never made it as a wise man; I couldn't cut it as a poor man stealing; tired of living like a blind man; I'm sick of sight without a sense of feeling, and this is how you remind me.

© 2001 WARNER-TAMERLANE PUBLISHING CORP., ARM YOUR DILLO PUBLISHING INC., BLACK DIESEL MUSIC, INC., ZERO G MUSIC INC. and LADEKIV MUSIC INC.
All Rights Administered by WARNER-TAMERLANE PUBLISHING CORP.
All Rights Reserved   Used by Permission

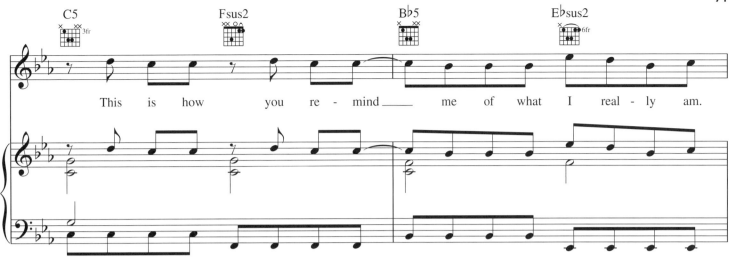

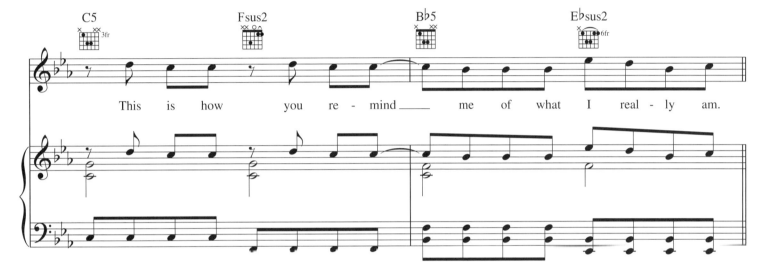

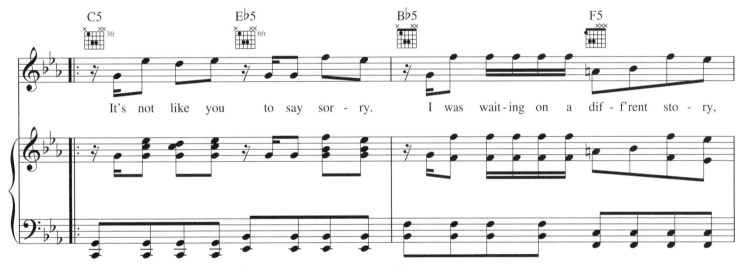

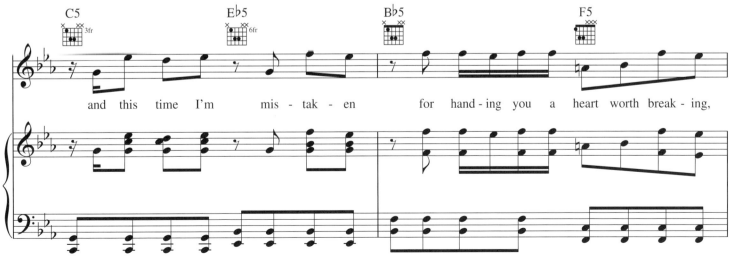

and I've been wrong, I've been down, been to the bot-tom of ev - 'ry bot - tle.

These five words __ in my head scream, "Are we hav - ing fun __ yet?" __

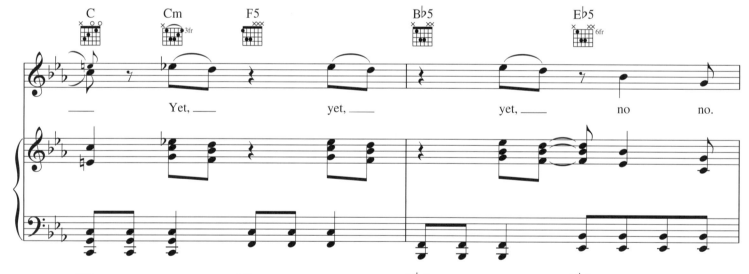

__ Yet, ___ yet, ___ yet, ___ no no.

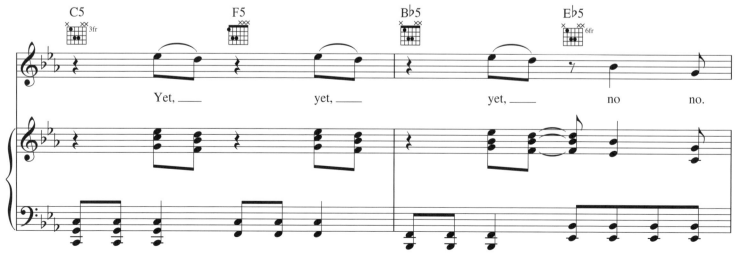

Yet, ___ yet, ___ yet, ___ no no.

It's not like ___ you did-n't know that. I said I love you, and I swear I still do.

And it must ___ have been so bad, 'cause liv-ing with him must have damn near killed you,

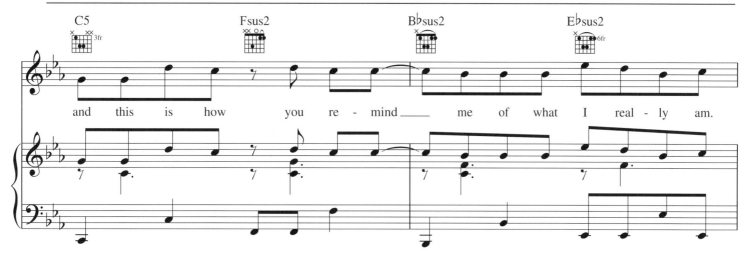

and this is how ___ you re-mind ___ me of what I real - ly am.

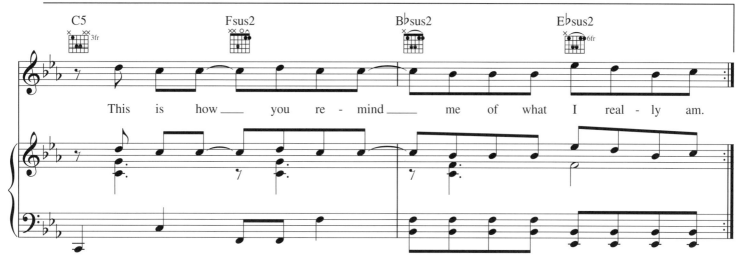

This is how ___ you re-mind ___ me of what I real - ly am.

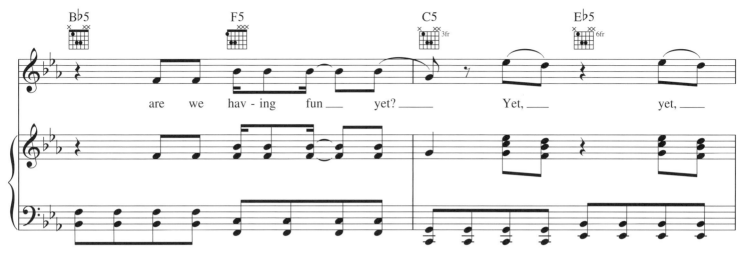

are we hav-ing fun ___ yet? ___ Yet, ___ yet, ___

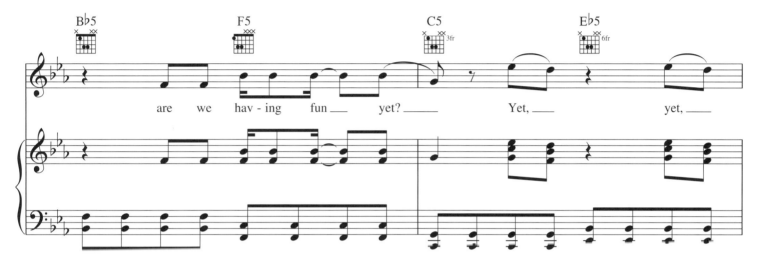

are we hav-ing fun ___ yet? ___ Yet, ___ yet, ___

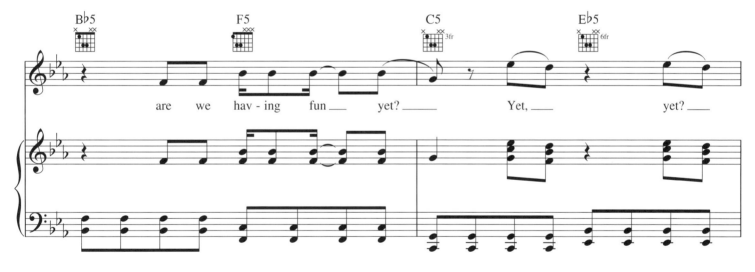

are we hav-ing fun ___ yet? ___ Yet, ___ yet? ___

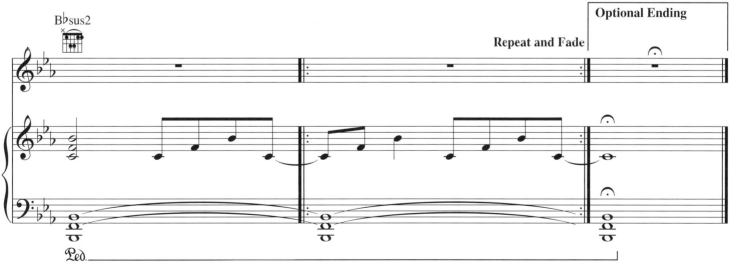

Repeat and Fade

Optional Ending

I'M LIKE A BIRD

Words and Music by
NELLY FURTADO

© 2000 NELSTAR PUBLISHING, INC.
All Rights Controlled and Administered by EMI APRIL MUSIC INC.
All Rights Reserved International Copyright Secured Used by Permission

love - ly, _____ but it's not for sure _____ that
pains me so much to tell _____ that

I won't ev - er _____ change. _____)
you don't know _____ me that well. _____)

And tho' my love is _____

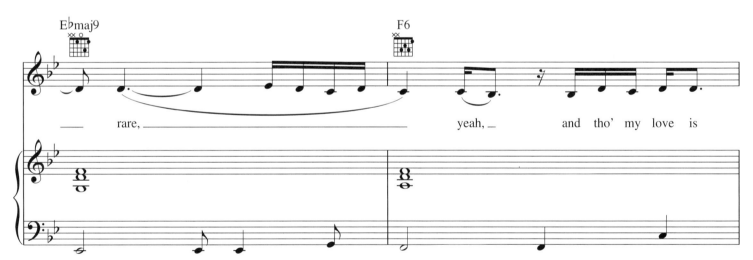

_____ rare, _____ yeah, _____ and tho' my love is

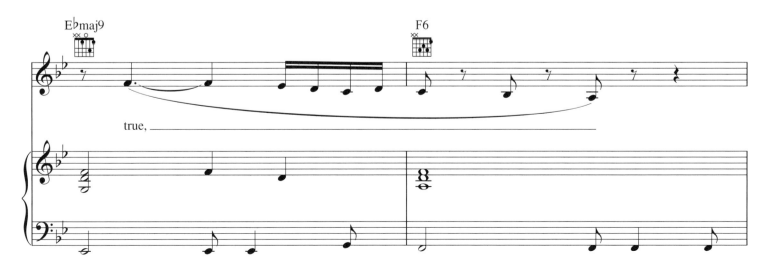

true, _____

give __ you __ a - way, __ yeah, yeah, yeah, __ yeah. __

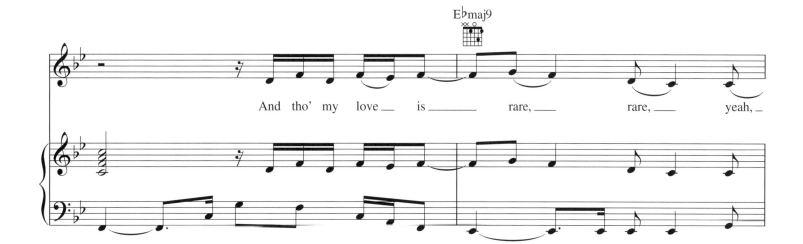

And tho' my love __ is __ rare, __ rare, __ yeah, __

__ yeah, _ and tho' my love __ is true, _____ yeah, _

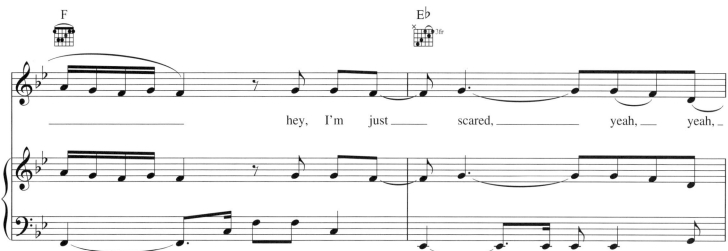

_____ hey, I'm just _____ scared, _____ yeah, __ yeah, __

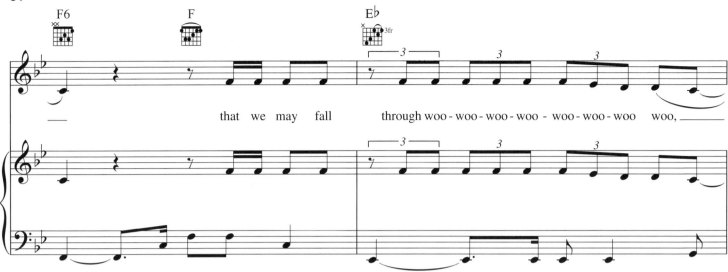

that we may fall through woo - woo - woo - woo - woo - woo - woo woo, _____

yeah, _____ yeah, yeah, _____ yeah. _____

I'm like _ a bird, _____ I _____ don't know _ where my

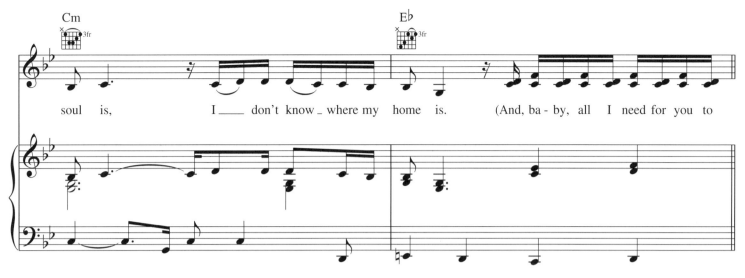

soul is, I ___ don't know _ where my home is. (And, ba - by, all I need for you to

I'm like _ a bird, ___ I'll on - ly fly a - way. ___ I ___ don't know _ where my
know is:)

Repeat ad lib. and Fade

soul is, I ___ don't know ___ where my home is. (And, ba - by, all I need for you to

LIFE IS A HIGHWAY

Words and Music by
TOM COCHRANE

Moderate Rock

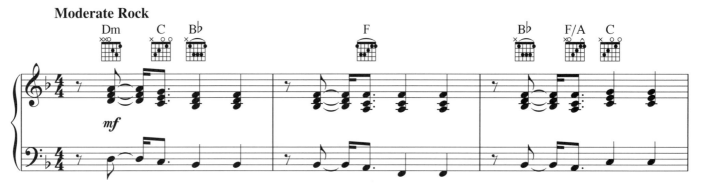

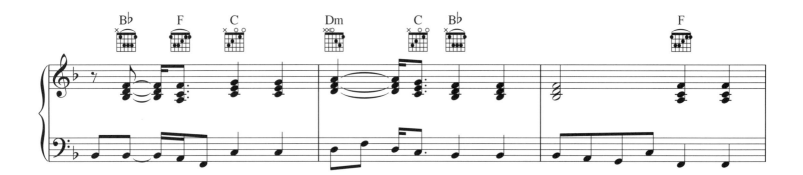

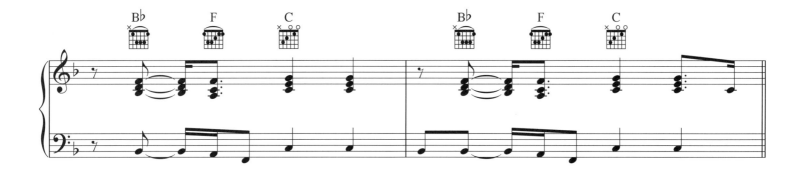

Life's like a road _ that you trav-el on when there's one _ day here _ and the next _ day gone. _ Some-times _
all these cit-ies and all these towns, it's in my blood _ and it's all _ a - round. _ I love _

Copyright © 1991 UNIVERSAL MUSIC PUBLISHING, A Division of UNIVERSAL MUSIC CANADA, INC.
All Rights in the U.S. and Canada Controlled and Administered by UNIVERSAL - POLYGRAM INTERNATIONAL PUBLISHING, INC.
All Rights Reserved   Used by Permission

you bend and some-times __ you stand. __ Some-times __ you turn __ your back __ to the wind. There's a world __
you now __ like I loved __ you then. __ This is the road and these __ are the hands. From Mo -

__ out - side __ ev -'ry dark - ened door __ where blues __ won't haunt __ you an - y - more. Where the
- zam - bique __ to those Mem - phis nights, __ the Khy - ber Pass to Van - cou-ver's lights.

brave are free __ and lov - ers soar, __ come ride __ with me __ to the dis - tant shore.
Knock me down, __ get back up a - gain, __ you're in _____ my blood. __ I'm not a lone - ly man.

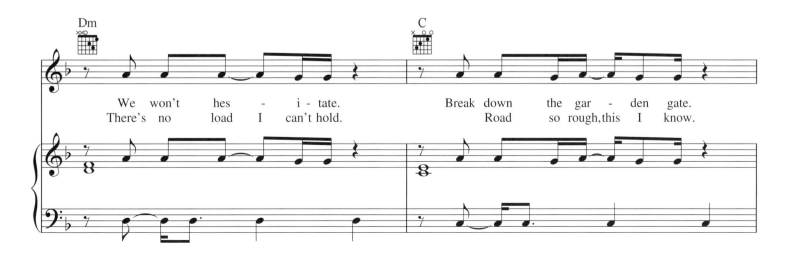

We won't hes - i - tate. Break down the gar - den gate.
There's no load I can't hold. Road so rough, this I know.

There's not much time left to-day. ___
I'll be there ___ when the light ___ comes in. ___ Just tell 'em we're ___ sur-vi-vors. ___

Life is a high-way. I ___ wan-na ride ___ it all ___ night long. ___

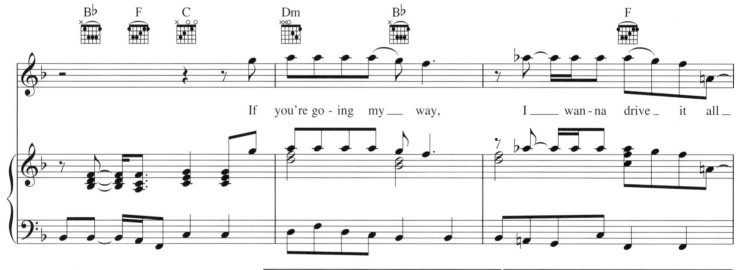

If you're go-ing my ___ way, I ___ wan-na drive ___ it all ___

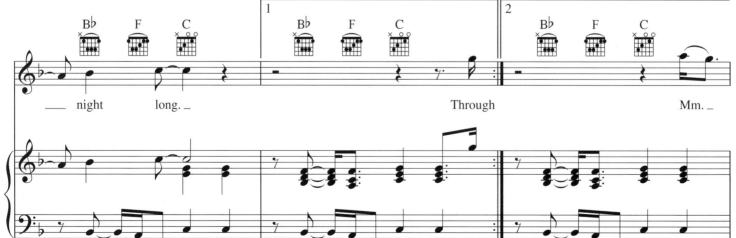

___ night long. ___ Through Mm. ___

Life is a high-way. I ___ wan-na ride ___ it all ___ night long. ___

Gim-me, gim-me, gim-me, gim-me yeah. If you're go-ing my ___ way,

I ___ wan-na drive ___ it all ___ night long. ___

There was a dis-tance be-tween you and I.

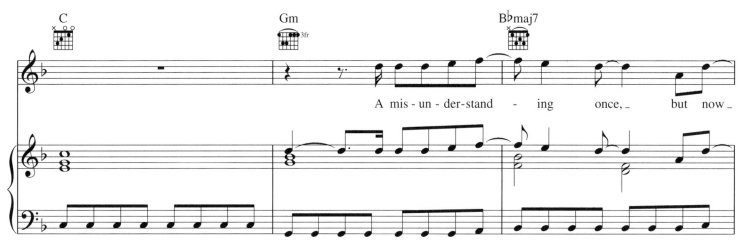

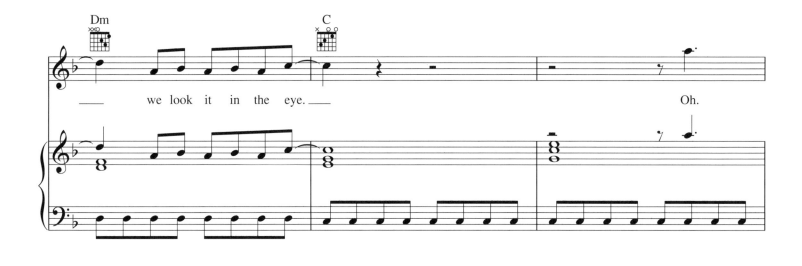

A mis-un-der-stand — ing once, _ but now _ we look it in the eye. _ Oh.

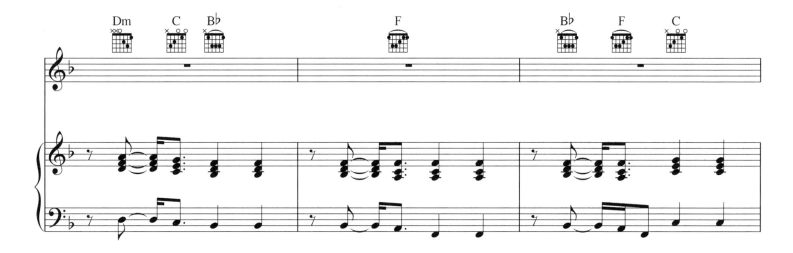

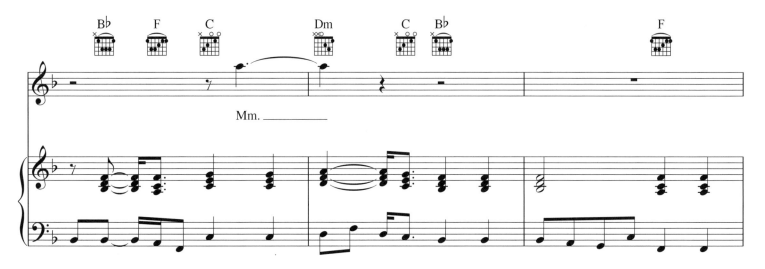

Mm. _

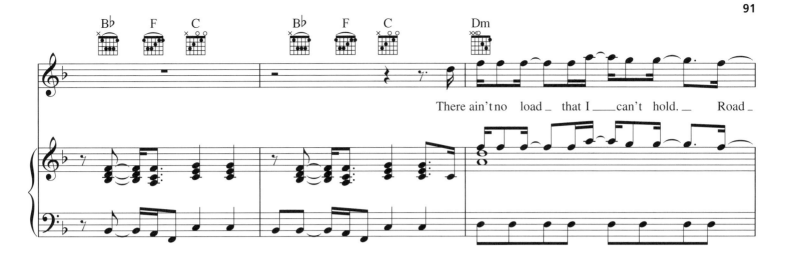

There ain't no load _ that I ___ can't hold. _ Road _

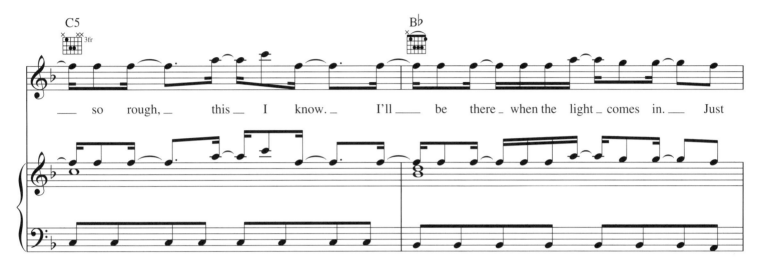

_ so rough, _ this _ I know. _ I'll _ be there _ when the light _ comes in. _ Just

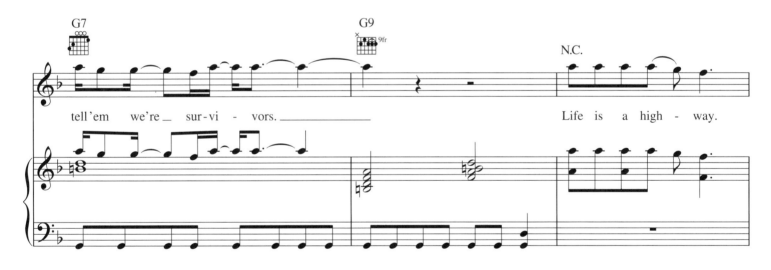

tell 'em we're _ sur-vi - vors. _____ Life is a high - way.

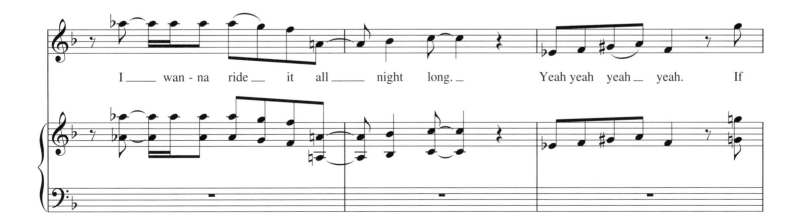

I ___ wan - na ride _ it all _ night long. _ Yeah yeah yeah _ yeah. If

you're go-ing my ___ way, I ___ wan-na drive ___ it all ___ night long. ___

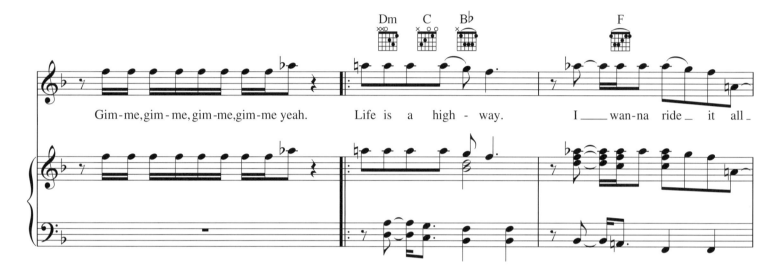

Gim-me, gim-me, gim-me, gim-me yeah. Life is a high-way. I ___ wan-na ride ___ it all ___

___ night long. ___ If you're go-ing my ___ way,

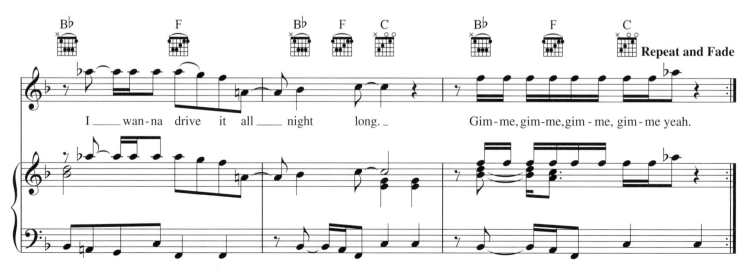

I ___ wan-na drive it all ___ night long. ___ Gim-me, gim-me, gim-me, gim-me yeah.

JUST LIKE YOU

Words and Music by THREE DAYS GRACE
and GAVIN BROWN

Heavy Rock

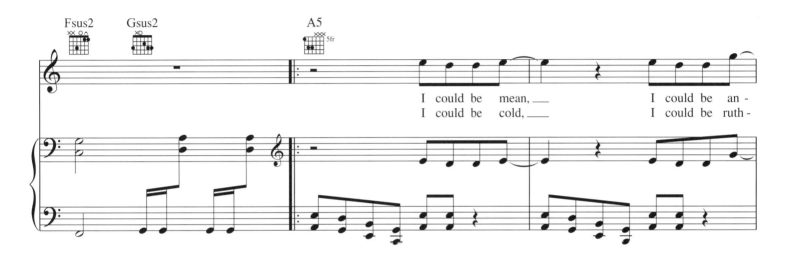

I could be mean, ___ I could be an -
I could be cold, ___ I could be ruth -

- gry.} You know I could be just like ___ you. ___   I could be fake, ___
- less.}   I could be weak, ___

___ I could be stu - pid.} You know I could be just like ___ you. ___
___ I could be sense - less.}

© 2003 EMI APRIL MUSIC (CANADA) LTD., 3 DAYS GRACE PUBLISHING and NOODLES FOR EVERYONE
All Rights in the U.S. Controlled and Administered by EMI APRIL MUSIC INC.
All Rights Reserved   International Copyright Secured   Used by Permission

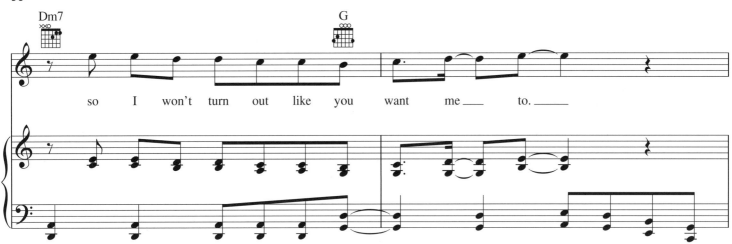

so I won't turn out like you want me ___ to. ___

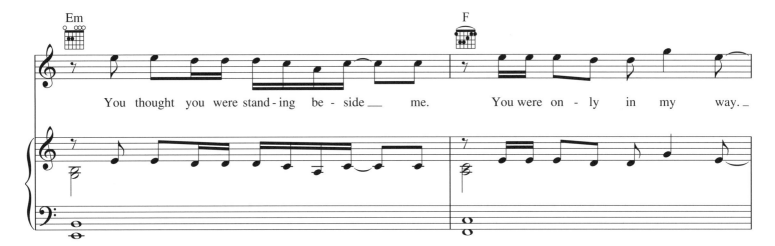

You thought you were stand-ing be-side ___ me. You were on-ly in my way. ___

___ You're wrong if you think that I'll ___ be just like ___ you. ___

You thought you were there to guide ___ me. You were on-ly in my way. ___

You're wrong if you think that I'll __ be just like __ you. __

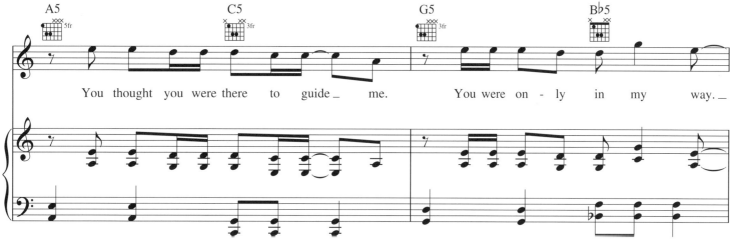

You thought you were there to guide __ me. You were on - ly in my way. __

__ You're wrong if you think that I'll __ be just like __ you. _____ I could be mean, __

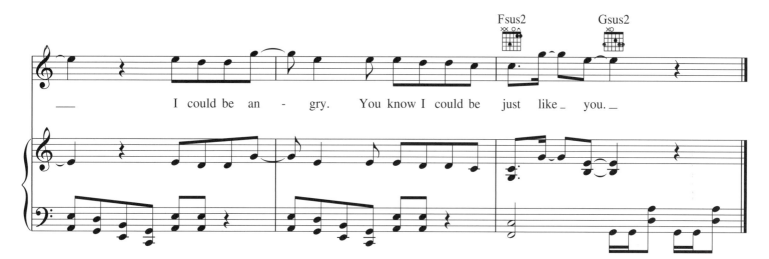

__ I could be an - gry. You know I could be just like __ you. __

MMM MMM MMM MMM

Words and Music by
BRAD ROBERTS

Copyright © 1993 UNIVERSAL - POLYGRAM INTERNATIONAL PUBLISHING, INC., DOOR NUMBER TWO MUSIC and DUMMIES PRODUCTIONS, INC.
All Rights Controlled and Administered by UNIVERSAL - POLYGRAM INTERNATIONAL PUBLISHING, INC.
All Rights Reserved   Used by Permission

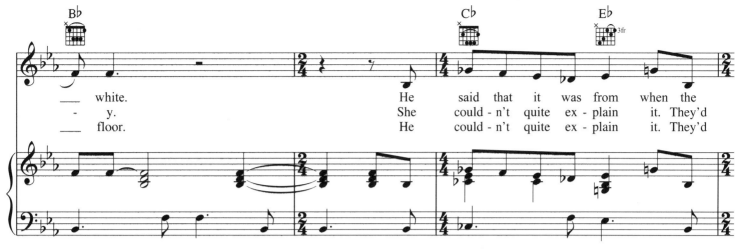

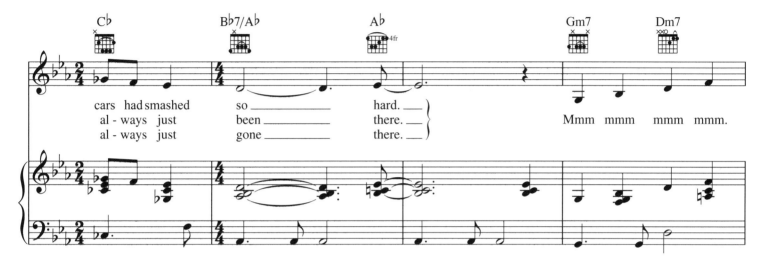

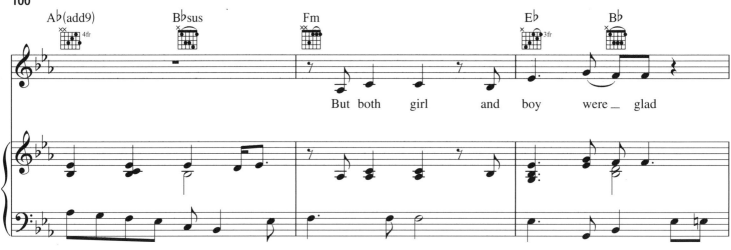

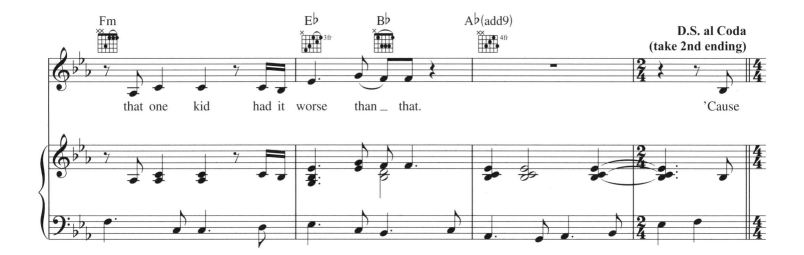

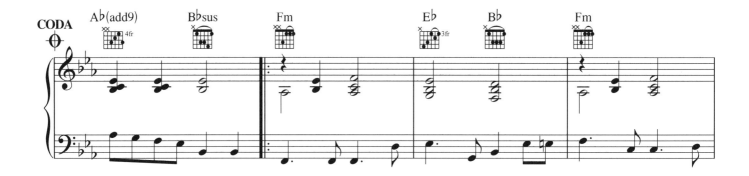

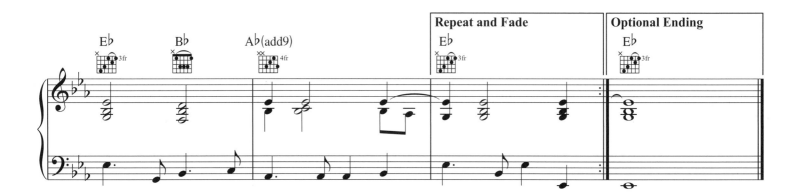

SUNDOWN

Words and Music by
GORDON LIGHTFOOT

Moderate Folk Rock

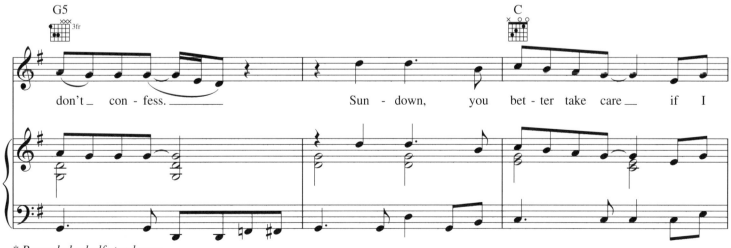

* Recorded a half step lower.

© 1973 (Renewed) MOOSE MUSIC LTD.
All Rights Reserved

find you been creep-in' 'round ___ my back stairs. ___ Sun - down, you

bet - ter take care ___ if I find you been creep-in' 'round ___ my back stairs. ___

She's been look - in' like a queen in a sail - or's dream ___ and she
see her look - in' fast in her fad - ed jeans. ___ She's a

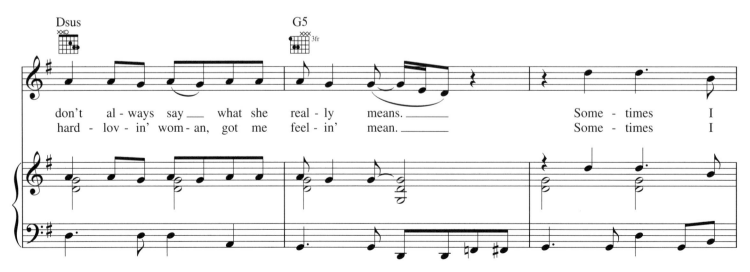

don't al - ways say ___ what she real - ly means. ___ Some - times I
hard - lov - in' wom - an, got me feel - in' mean. ___ Some - times I

think it's a shame __ when I get feel - in' bet - ter when I'm feel - in' no pain. __
think it's a shame __ when I get feel - in' bet - ter when I'm feel - in' no pain. __

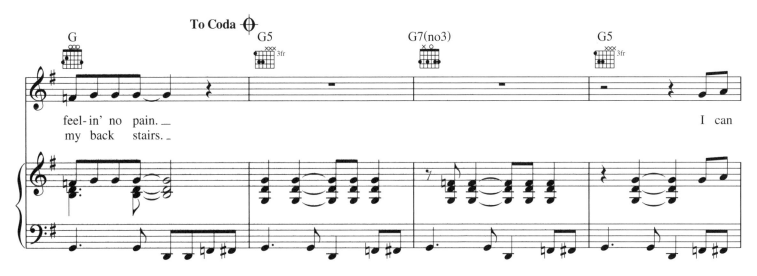

Some - times I think it's a shame __ when I get feel - in' bet - ter when I'm
Sun - down, you bet - ter take care __ if I find you been creep - in' 'round __

To Coda

feel - in' no pain. __ I can
my back stairs. __

pic - ture ev - 'ry move that a man could make, __ gett - ing lost in her lov - ing is your

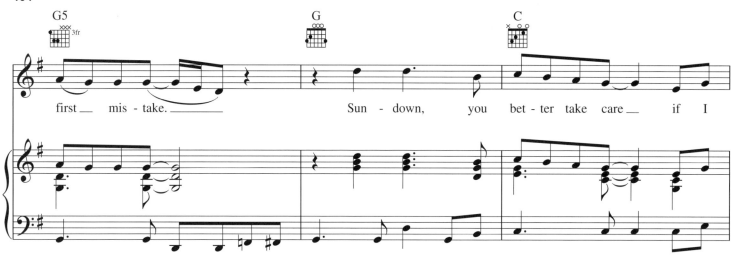

first __ mis - take. _____ Sun - down, you bet - ter take care __ if I

find you been creep - in' 'round __ my back stairs. __ Some - times I

think it's a sin __ when I feel like I'm win - nin' when I'm los - in' a - gain. __

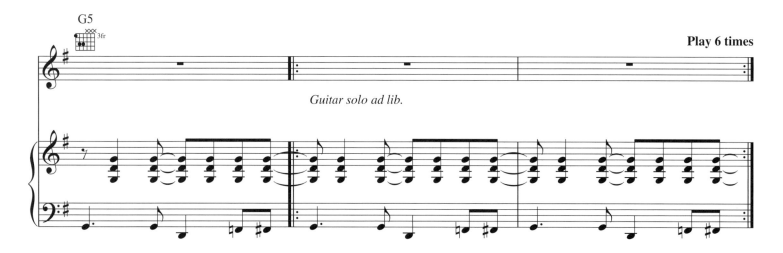

Play 6 times

Guitar solo ad lib.

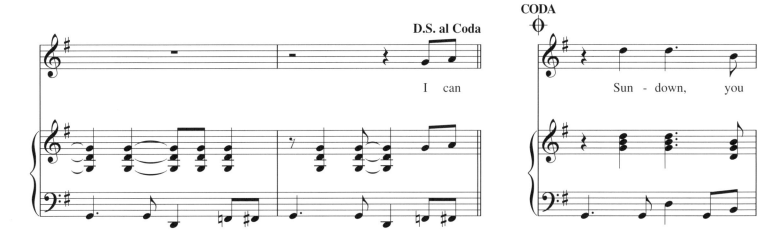

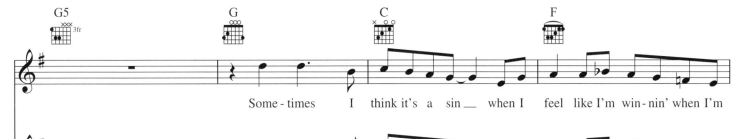

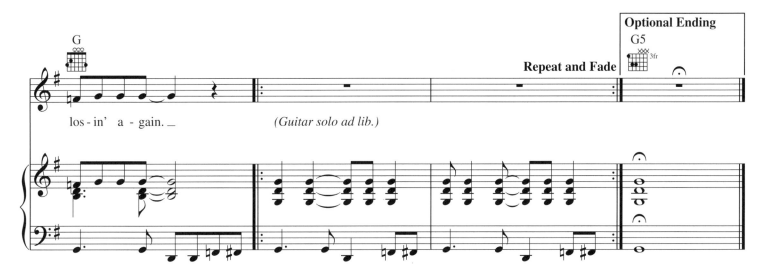

1, 2, 3, 4

Words and Music by FEIST
and SALLY SELTMANN

Copyright © 2007 by Universal Music Publishing MGB Ltd. and Songs of SMP
All Rights for Universal Music Publishing MGB Ltd. in the U.S. and Canada Administered by Universal Music - MGB Songs
International Copyright Secured   All Rights Reserved

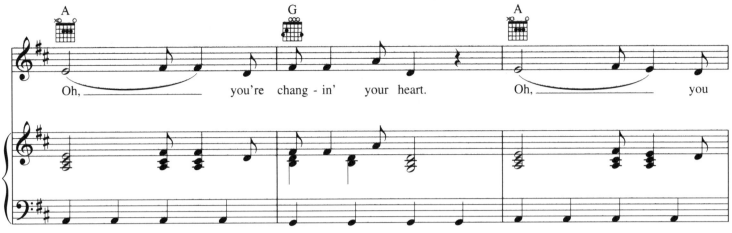

Oh, _____ you're chang-in' your heart. Oh, _____ you

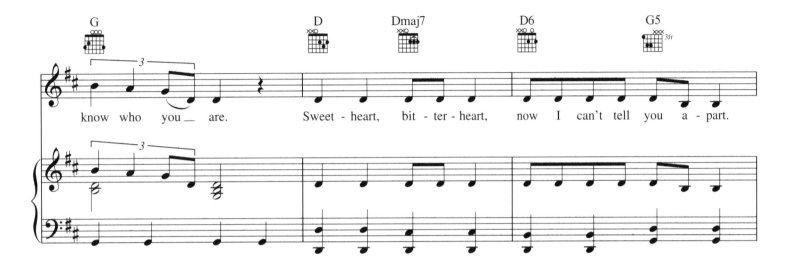

know who you ___ are. Sweet - heart, bit - ter - heart, now I can't tell you a - part.

Co - zy and cold, ___ put the horse be - fore the cart. Those teen - age ___ hopes ___ who have

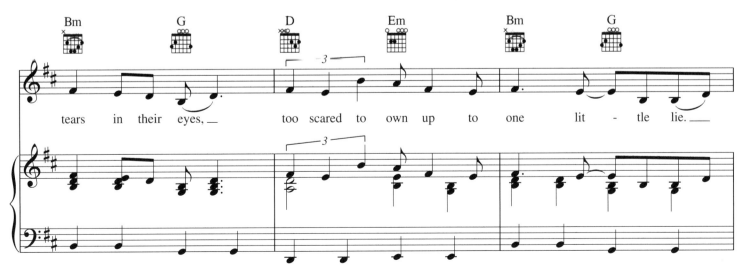

tears in their eyes, ___ too scared to own up to one lit - tle lie. ___

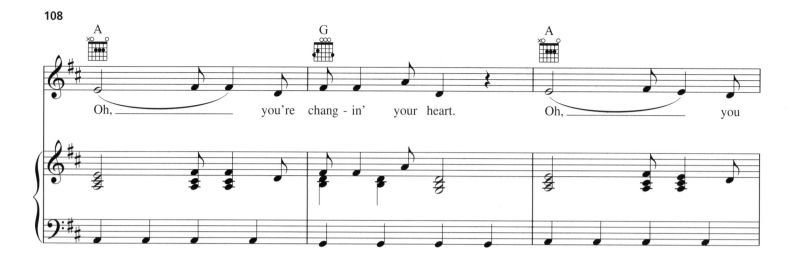

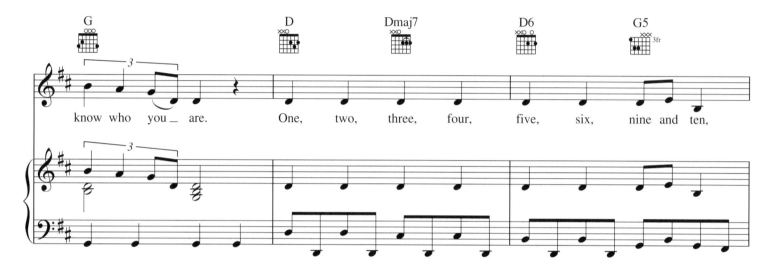

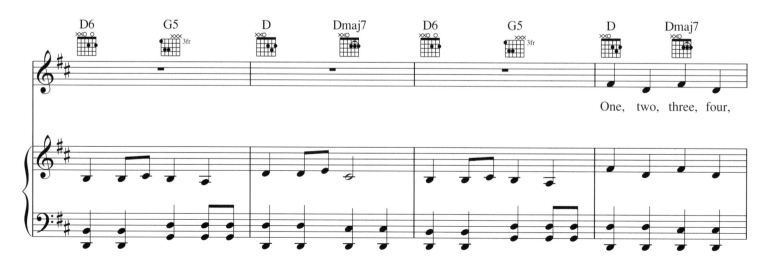

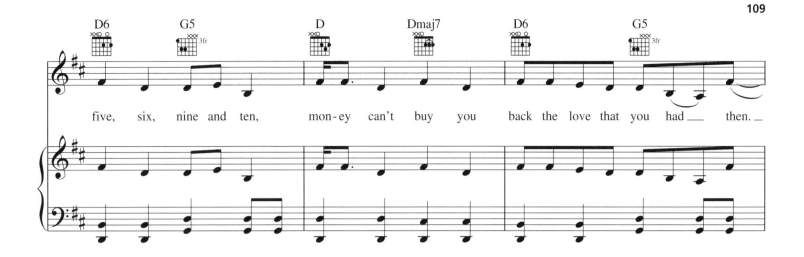

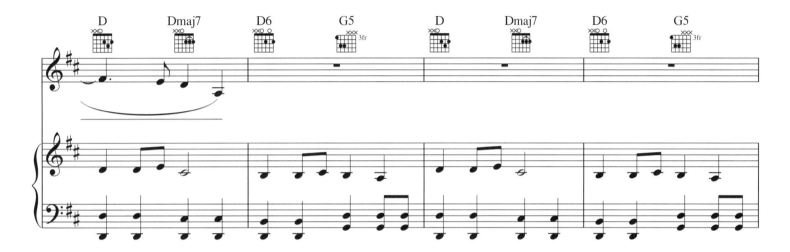

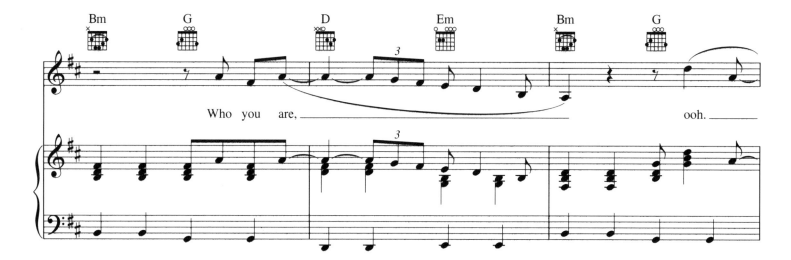

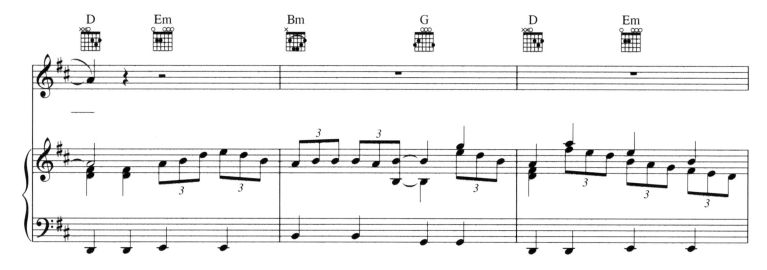

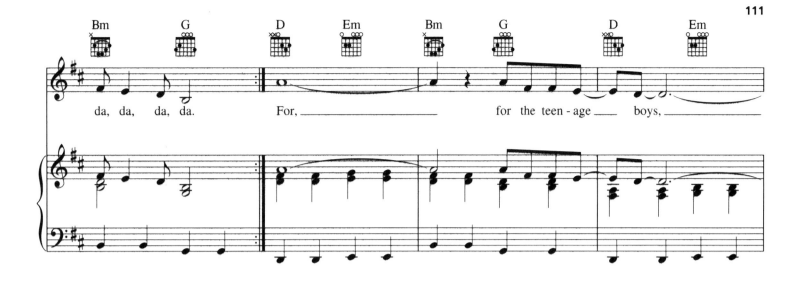

da, da, da, da. For, _____ for the teen-age ___ boys, ___

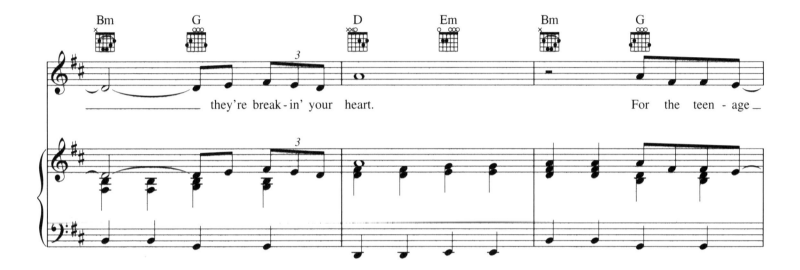

_____ they're break-in' your heart. For the teen-age __

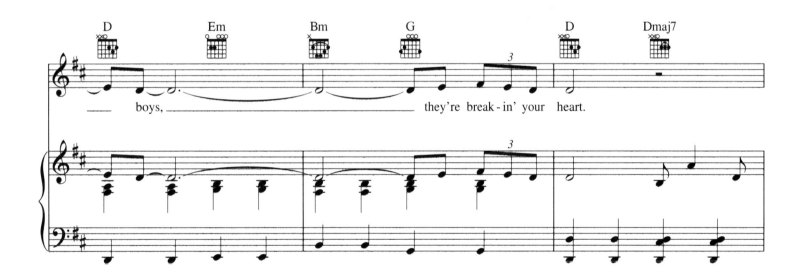

___ boys, _____ they're break-in' your heart.

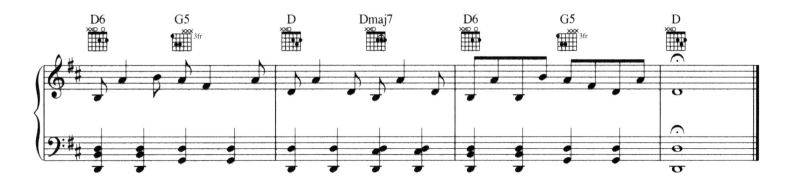

ONE WEEK

Words and Music by
ED ROBERTSON

It's been one week since you looked at me, ____ cocked your head to one side _ and said, "I'm an-gry." Five days since you laughed at me, _ say-ing, "Get that to-geth-er, come _ back and see me." Three days since the liv-ing room. _ I

© 1998 WB MUSIC CORP. and TREAT BAKER MUSIC
All Rights Administered by WB MUSIC CORP.
All Rights Reserved   Used by Permission

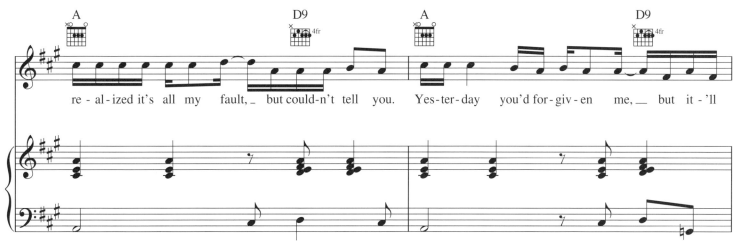

re-al-ized it's all my fault, _ but could-n't tell you. Yes-ter-day you'd for-giv-en me, _ but it-'ll

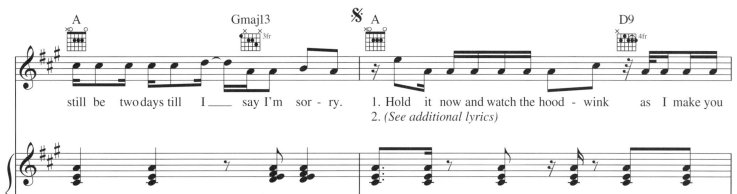

still be two days till I ___ say I'm sor-ry. 1. Hold it now and watch the hood - wink as I make you
2. *(See additional lyrics)*

stop, think. You'll think you're look-ing at Aq - ua - man.

I sum-mon fish to the dish, al-though I like the Cha - let

Tryin' hard not to smile, though I feel bad.

I'm the kind of guy who laughs at a fu-ner-al.

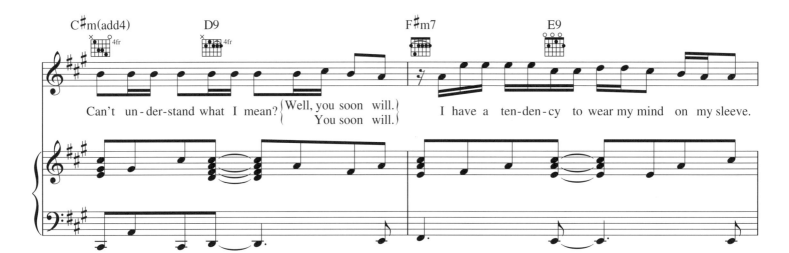

Can't un-der-stand what I mean? {Well, you soon will.} {You soon will.} I have a ten-den-cy to wear my mind on my sleeve.

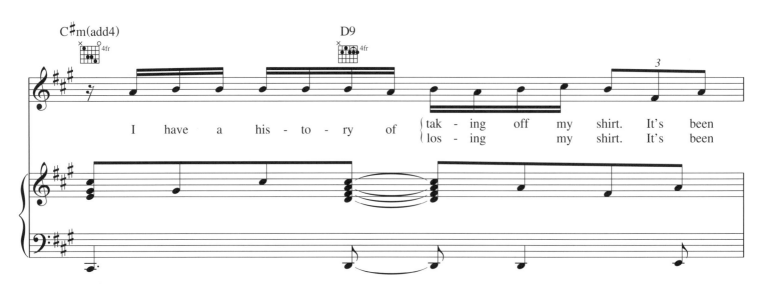

I have a his-to-ry of {tak-ing off my shirt. It's been} {los-ing my shirt. It's been}

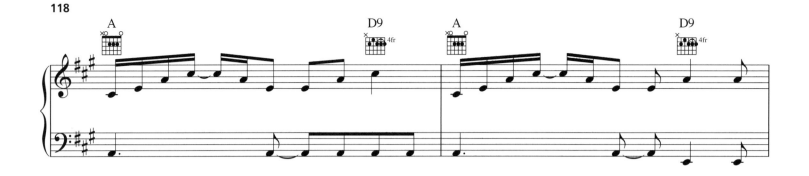

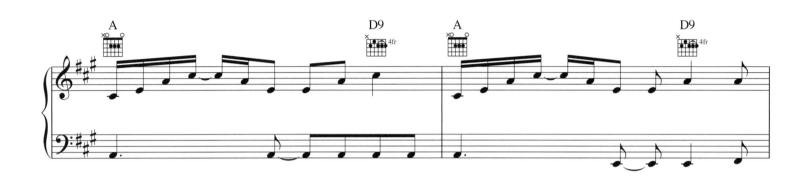

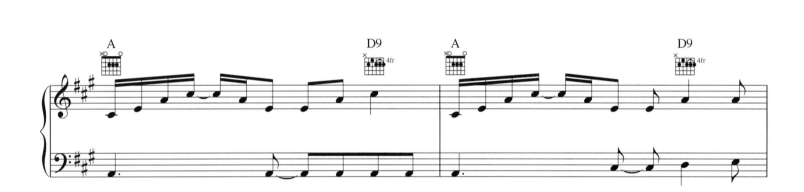

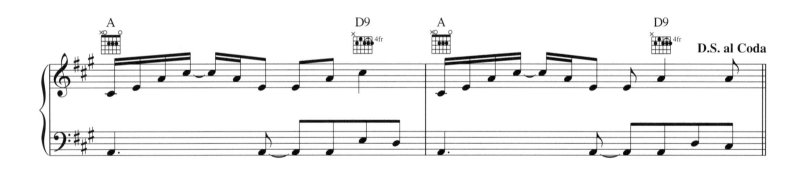

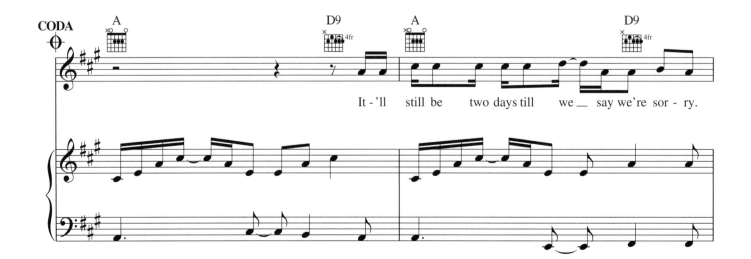

It -'ll still be two days till we __ say we're sor - ry.

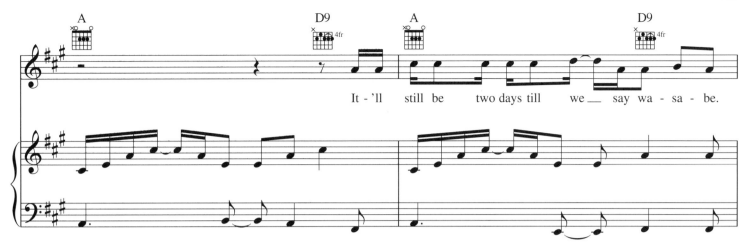

It-'ll still be two days till we __ say wa-sa-be.

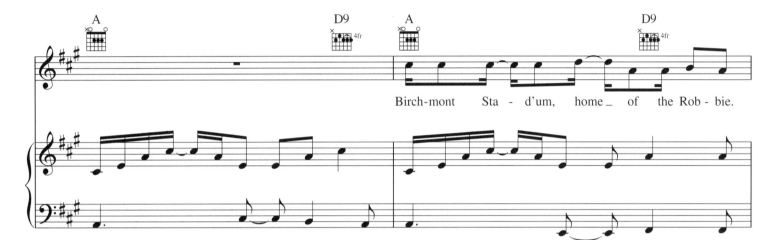

Birch-mont Sta - d'um, home __ of the Rob - bie.

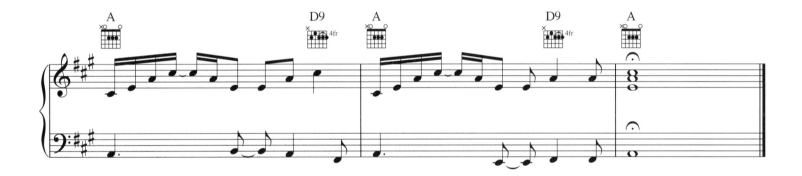

Additional Lyrics

2. Chickity China the Chinese chicken,
Have a drumstick and your brain stops tickin'.
Watchin' "X-Files" with no lights on.
We're *dans la maison*.
I hope the Smoking Man's in this one.
Like Harrison Ford, I'm getting frantic.
Like Sting, I'm tantric.
Like Snickers, guaranteed to satisfy.
Like Kurasawa, I make mad films.
OK, I don't make files,
But if I did, they'd have a Samurai.
Gonna get a set a'better clubs;
Gonna find the kind with tiny nubs
Just so my irons aren't always flying
Off the backswing.
Gotta get in tune with Sailor Moon,
'Cause the cartoon has got
The boom Anime babes
That make me think the wrong thing.
To Bridge

SOMEWHERE OUT THERE

Words and Music by RAINE MAIDA,
JEREMY TAGGART and DUNCAN COUTTS

Last time I talked — to you, — you were lone-ly and out of place. —
Down here in the at-mos-phere, _____ gar-bage and cit-y lights. —

You were look-in' down — on me, — lost out in space. —
You've gone to save your tired ____ soul. — You've gone to save our lives. —

Recorded a half step lower.

Copyright © 2002 Sony/ATV Music Publishing Canada, Under Zenith Publishing, I'm In Zihuatanejo Music and Two Months In The Hole
All Rights Administered by Sony/ATV Music Publishing, 8 Music Square West, Nashville, TN 37203
International Copyright Secured   All Rights Reserved

We laid un-der-neath the stars _ strung out and feel-ing brave. _
I turned on the ra - di - o _ to find you on sat-el - lite. _

Watched the red - or'nge glow. I watched it float a - way. _
I'm wait - ing for this sky _ to fall. _ I'm wait - ing for a sign. _ And

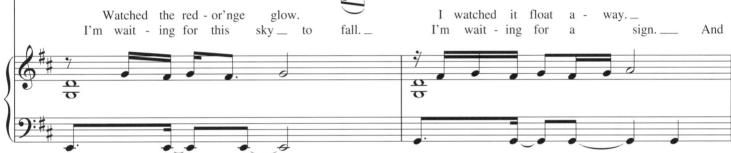

all we _ are _ is

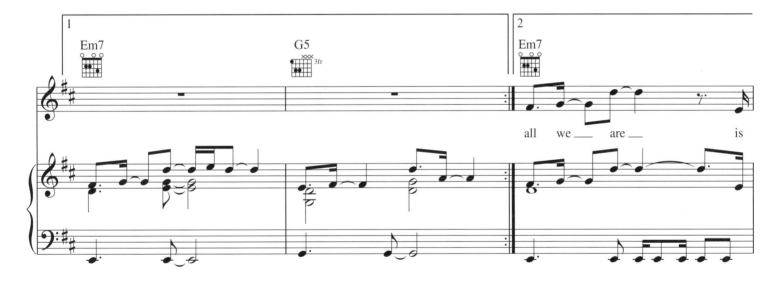

all so _ far. _ You're fall - ing back _ to

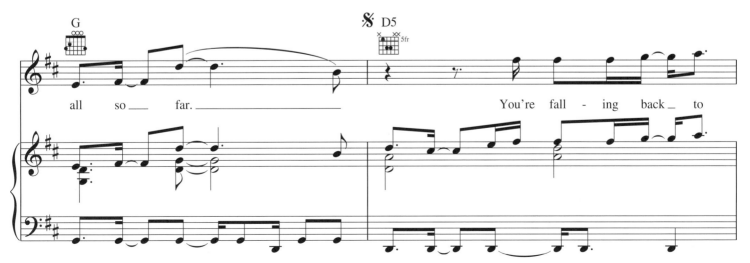

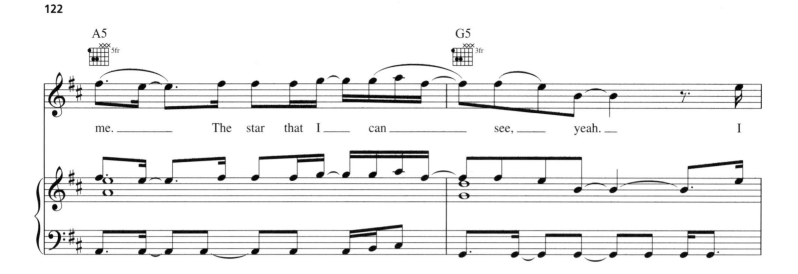

me. _____ The star that I ___ can _____ see, ____ yeah. ___ I

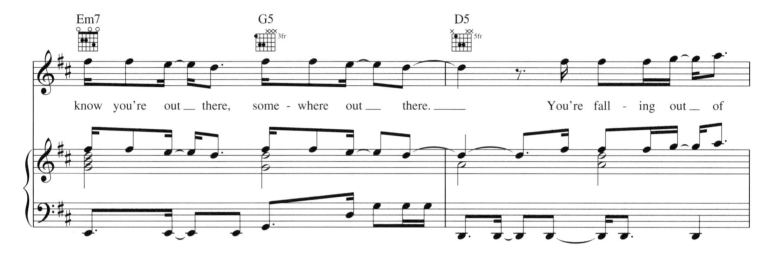

know you're out ___ there, some - where out ___ there. _____ You're fall - ing out ___ of

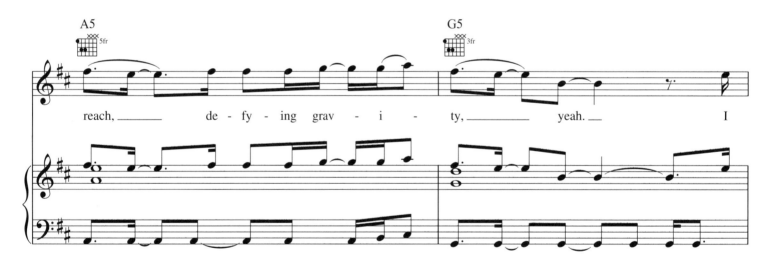

reach, _____ de - fy - ing grav - i ___ - ty, _____ yeah. ___ I

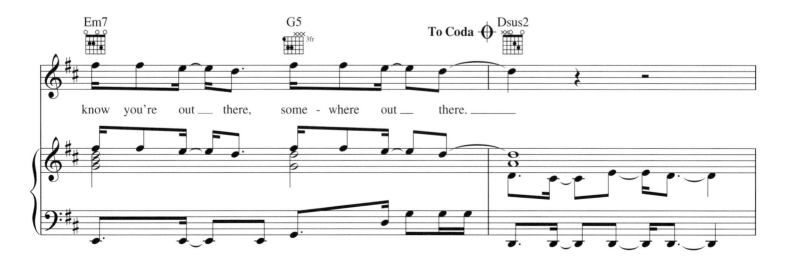

know you're out ___ there, some - where out ___ there. _____

Hope you re - mem - ber me __ when you're home - sick and need a change. __

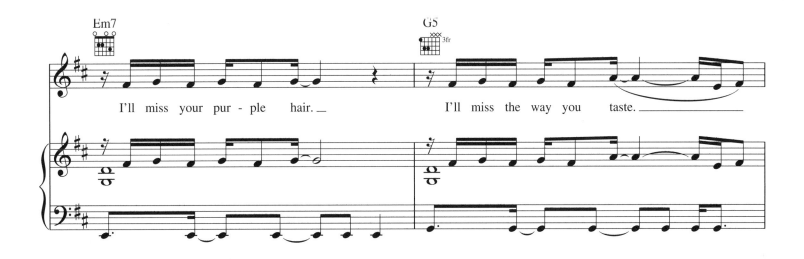

I'll miss your pur - ple hair. __ I'll miss the way you taste. __

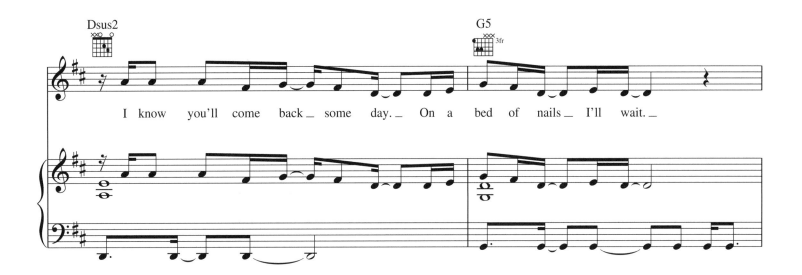

I know you'll come back __ some day. __ On a bed of nails __ I'll wait. __

I'm pray - in' that you don't _ burn out or fade _ a - way. ____ And

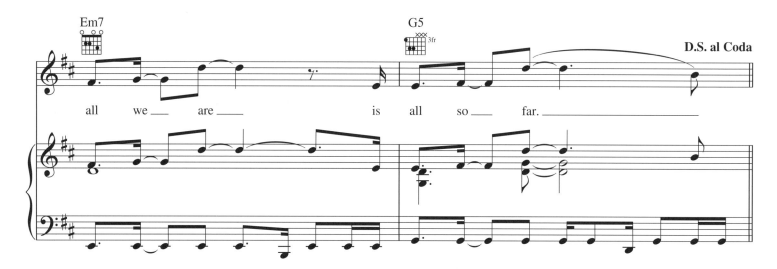

all we _ are ____ is all so _ far. _____

D.S. al Coda

CODA

____ me. ____ The star that I _ can _ see. ___

You're fall - ing back _ to

N.C.

me. ____ The star that I ___ can ___ see. ___ I know you're out _ there, _ ooh. _

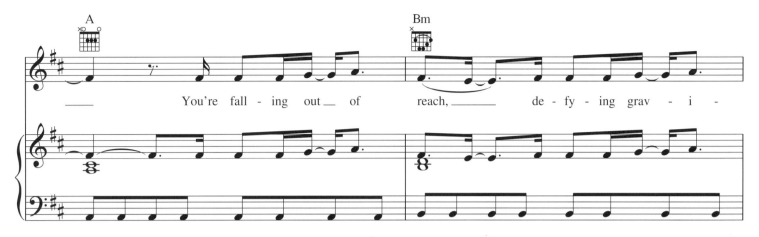

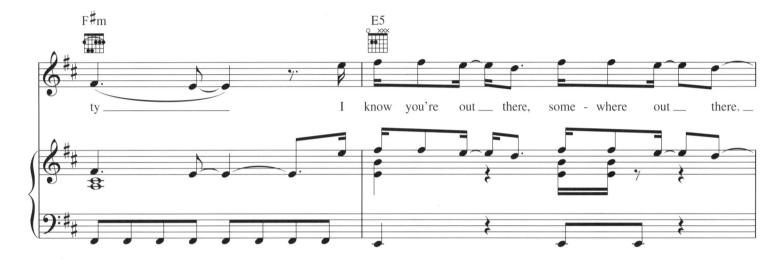

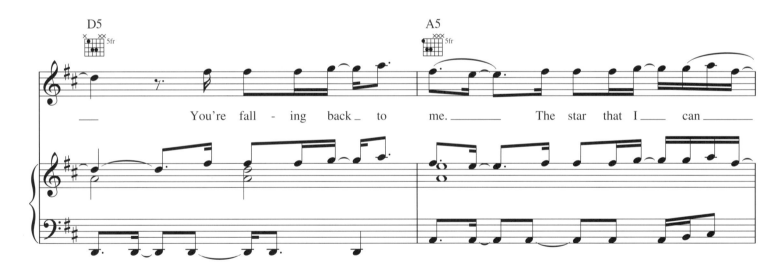

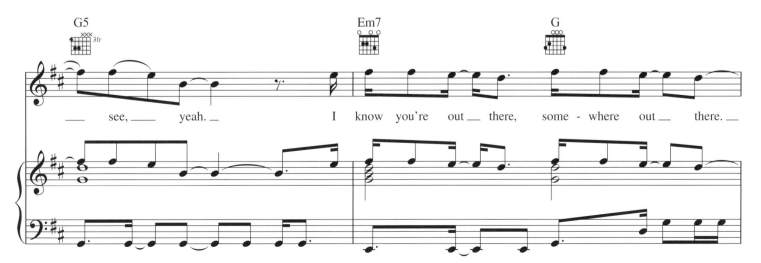

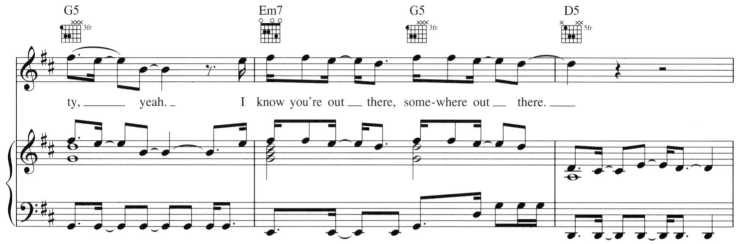

YOU AIN'T SEEN NOTHIN' YET

Words and Music by
RANDY BACHMAN

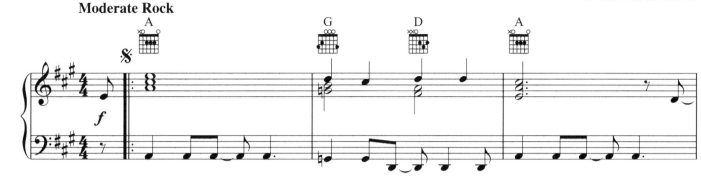

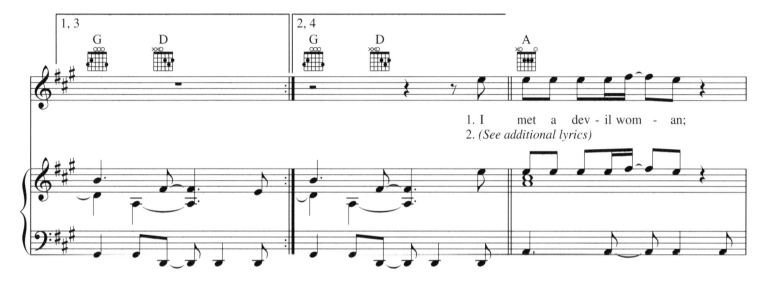

1. I met a dev - il wom - an;
2. (See additional lyrics)

she took my heart a - way. ___ She

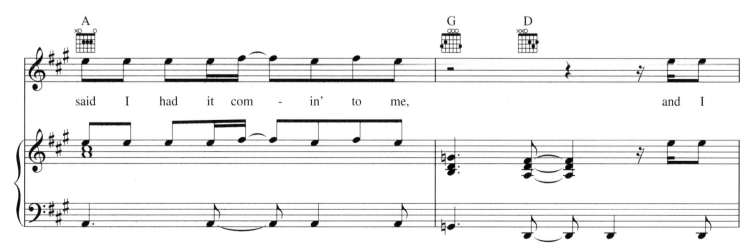

said I had it com - in' to me, and I

Copyright © 1974 Sony/ATV Music Publishing LLC
Copyright Renewed
All Rights Administered by Sony/ATV Music Publishing LLC, 8 Music Square West, Nashville, TN 37203
International Copyright Secured   All Rights Reserved

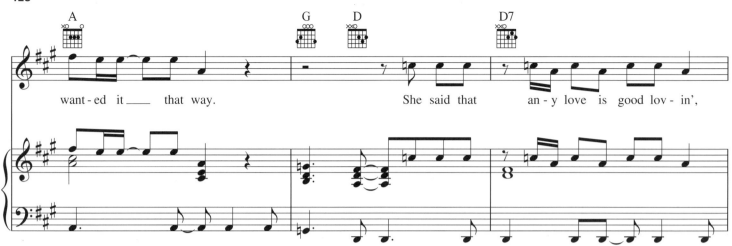

want-ed it ____ that way. She said that an - y love is good lov - in',

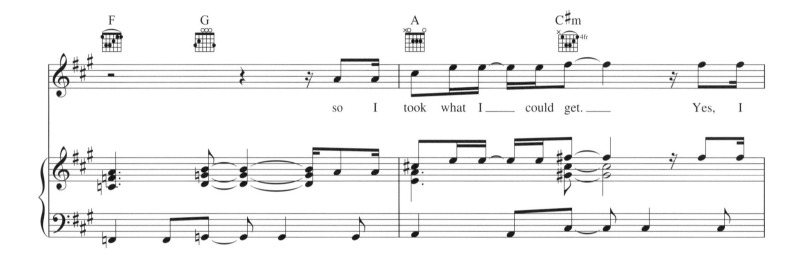

so I took what I ____ could get. ____ Yes, I

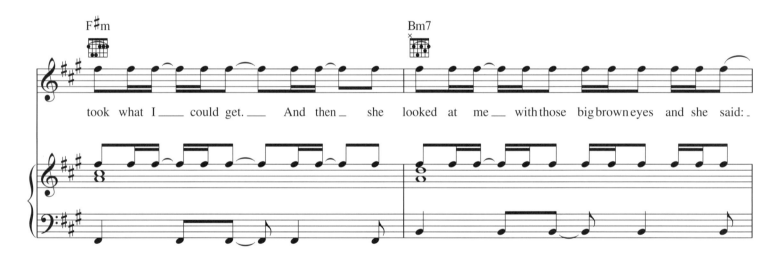

took what I ____ could get. ____ And then ____ she looked at me ____ with those big brown eyes and she said: ____

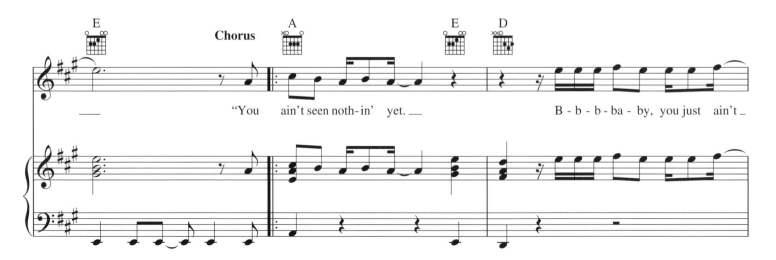

____ "You ain't seen noth-in' yet. ____ B - b - b - ba - by, you just ain't ____

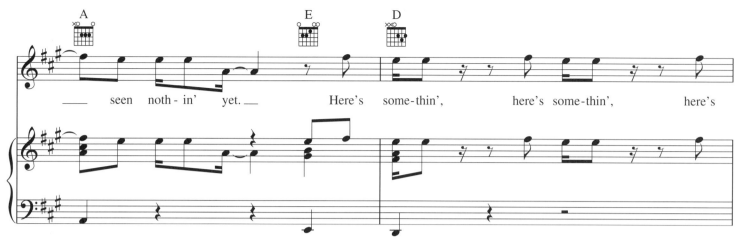

____ seen noth-in' yet. ____ Here's some-thin', here's some-thin', here's

some-thin' you ain't nev-er gon-na for-get, ba-by. Ya know, ___ ya know, ya know, you know you just

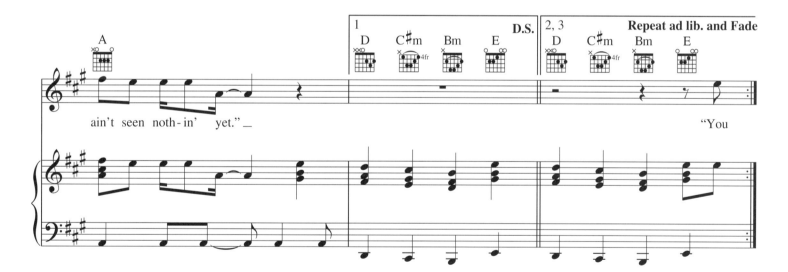

ain't seen noth-in' yet." ____ "You

Additional Lyrics

2. And now I'm feelin' better
   'Cause I found out for sure;
   She took me to her doctor
   And he told me of a cure.
   He said that
   Any love is good love,
   So I took what I could get.
   She looked at me with big brown eyes
   And said:
   Chorus

THESE EYES

Written by BURTON CUMMINGS
and RANDY BACHMAN

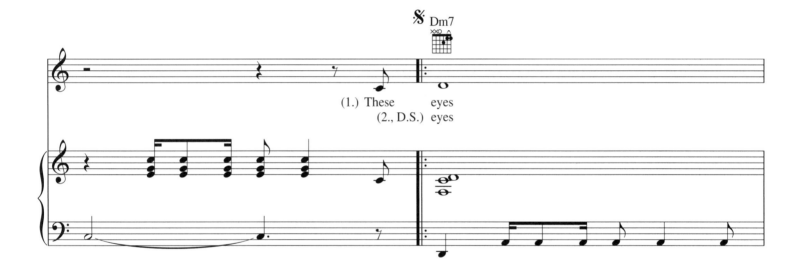

© 1969 (Renewed 1997) SHILLELAGH MUSIC (BMI)/Administered by BUG MUSIC, INC., A BMG CHRYSALIS COMPANY
All Rights Reserved   Used by Permission

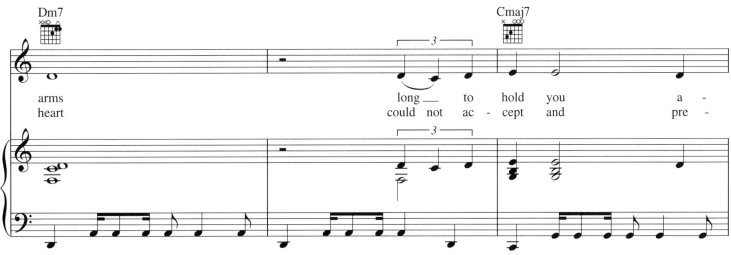

arms / heart
long ___ to hold you a- / could not ac- cept and pre-

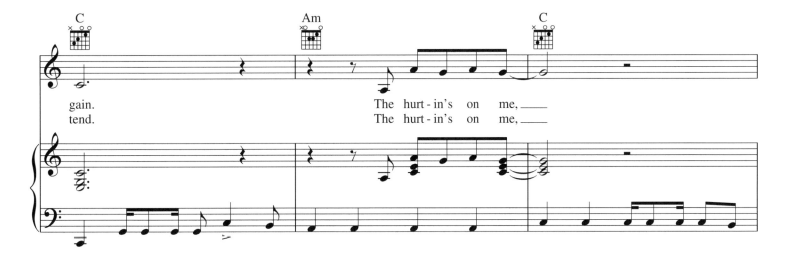

gain. / tend.
The hurt-in's on me, ___ / The hurt-in's on me, ___

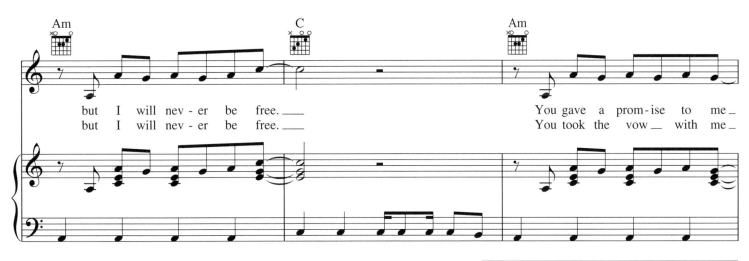

but I will nev-er be free. ___ / but I will nev-er be free. ___
You gave a prom-ise to me ___ / You took the vow ___ with me ___

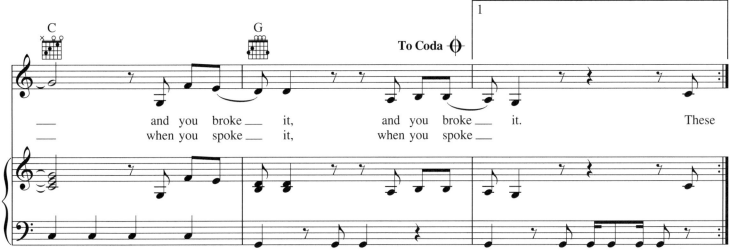

To Coda ⊕

1

___ and you broke ___ it, and you broke ___ it. These
when you spoke ___ it, when you spoke ___ it.

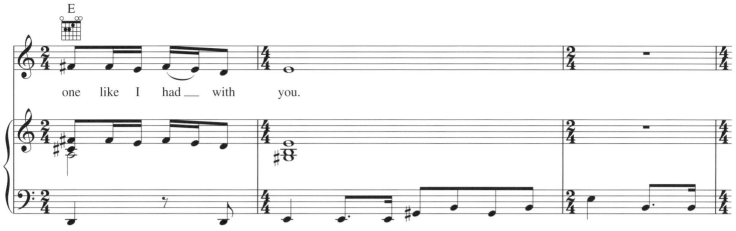

one like I had with you.

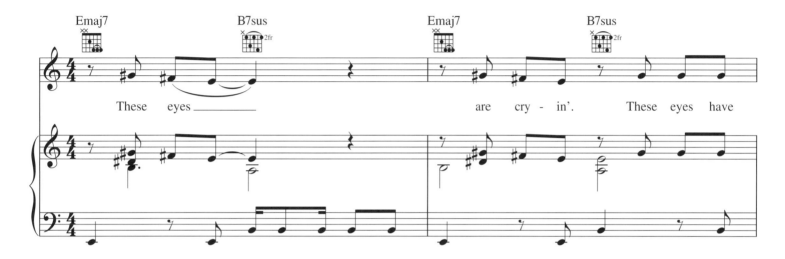

These eyes are cry - in'. These eyes have

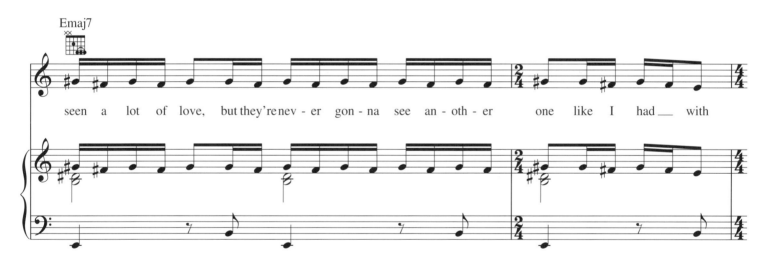

seen a lot of love, but they're nev - er gon - na see an - oth - er one like I had with

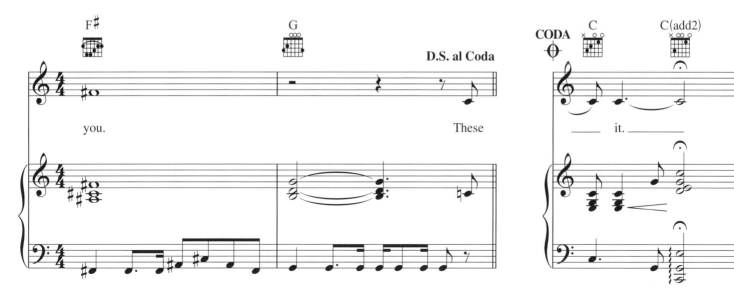

you. These it.

THIS COULD BE THE NIGHT

Words and Music by PAUL DEAN, MIKE RENO,
BILL WRAY and JONATHAN CAIN

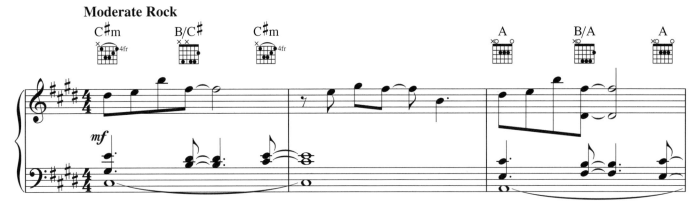

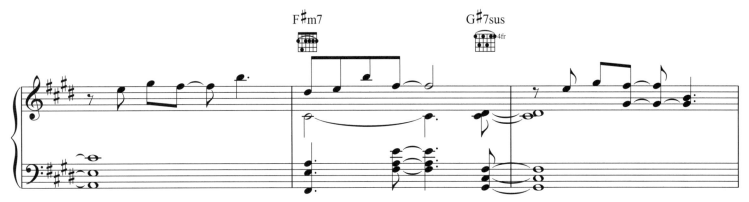

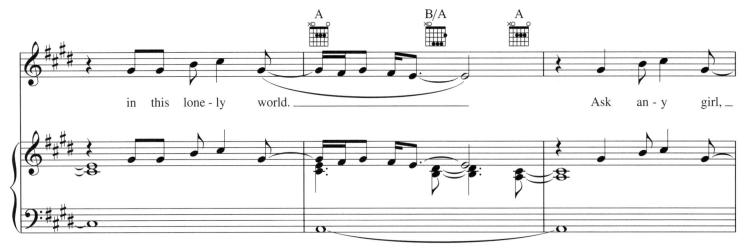

© 1985 EMI BLACKWOOD MUSIC (CANADA) LTD., DEAN OF MUSIC, EMI APRIL MUSIC (CANADA) LTD., DUKE RENO MUSIC, MEL-DAVIS MUSIC INC. and FRISCO KID MUSIC
All Rights for EMI BLACKWOOD MUSIC (CANADA) LTD. and DEAN OF MUSIC Controlled and Administered by EMI BLACKWOOD MUSIC INC.
All Rights for EMI APRIL MUSIC (CANADA) LTD. and DUKE RENO MUSIC Controlled and Administered by EMI APRIL MUSIC INC.
All Rights Reserved   International Copyright Secured   Used by Permission

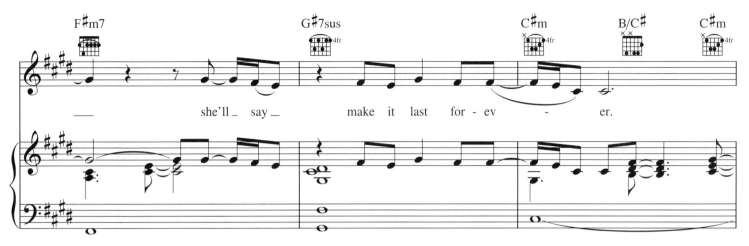

she'll _ say _ make it last for - ev - er.

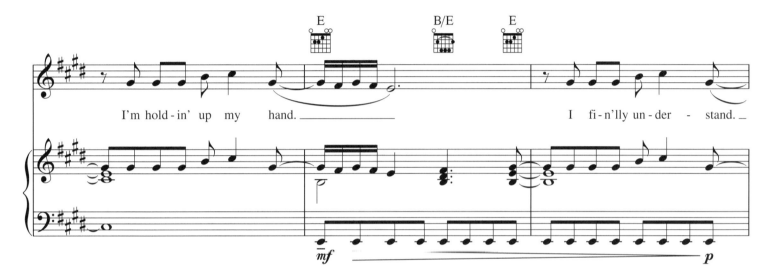

I'm hold - in' up my hand. _____ I fi - n'lly un - der - stand. _

So, turn out the lights, ____ oh, __ yeah. _

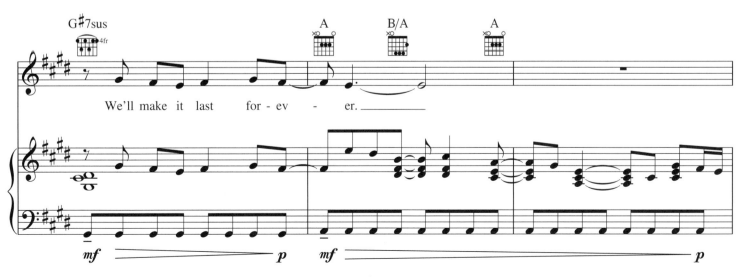

We'll make it last for - ev - er. _____

Out on the bor-der - line, _____

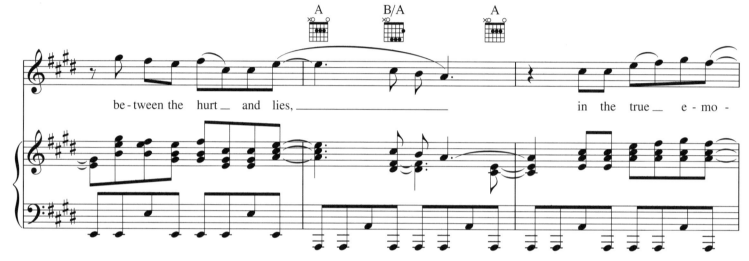

be - tween the hurt __ and lies, _____ in the true __ e - mo -

- tions _____ that make it last for - ev - er.

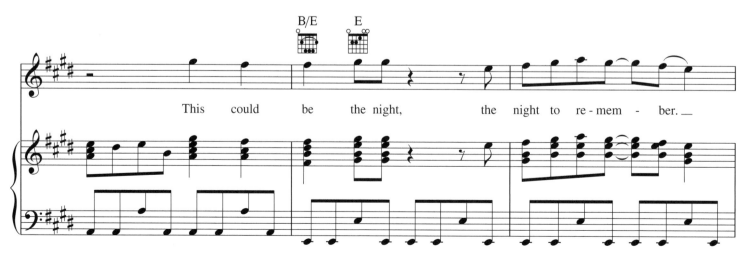

This could be the night, the night to re - mem - ber. __

We'll make it last ___ for-ev ___ -er. This could be the night, ___ oh, ___

___ to end all night. ___

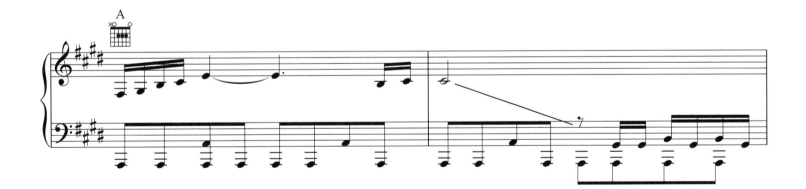

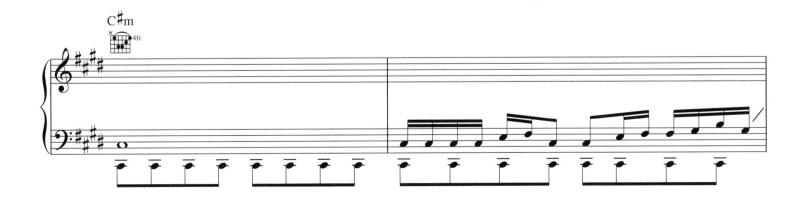

D.S. al Coda

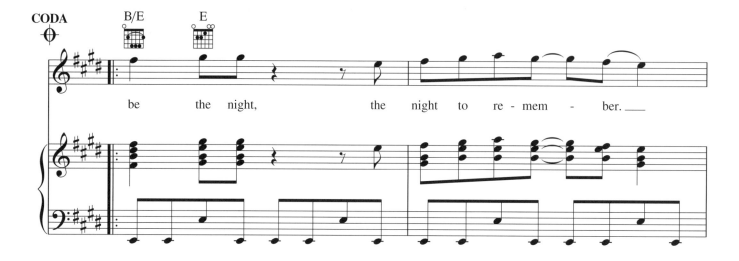

be the night, the night to re - mem - ber. ___

We'll make it last ___ for - ev - er. This could

be the night, oh, ___ to end all

TOM SAWYER

Words by PYE DUBOIS and NEIL PEART
Music by GEDDY LEE and ALEX LIFESON

mod-ern day war-ri-or, mean, mean stride. To-day's Tom Saw-yer, mean, ___ mean ___ pride.

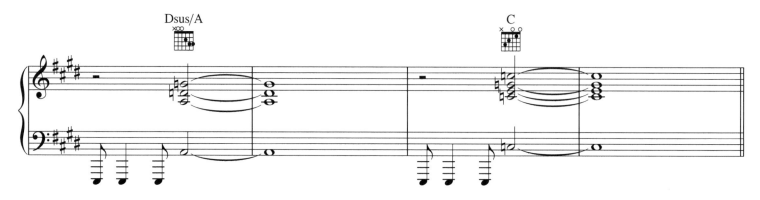

© 1981 CORE MUSIC PUBLISHING
All Rights Reserved   Used by Permission

Though his mind is not ___ for rent don't put him
No, his mind is not ___ for rent to an - y

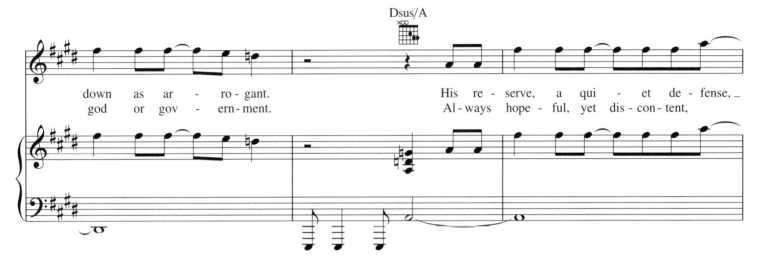

down as ar - ro - gant. His re - serve, a qui - et de - fense, ___
god or gov - ern - ment. Al - ways hope - ful, yet dis - con - tent,

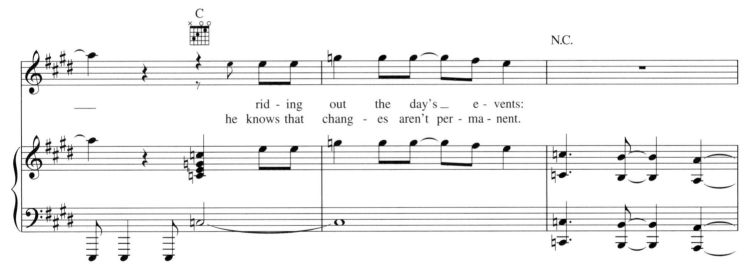

___ rid - ing out the day's ___ e - vents:
he knows that chang - es aren't per - ma - nent.

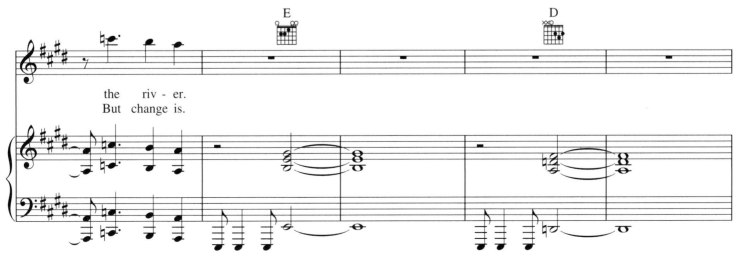

the riv - er.
But change is.

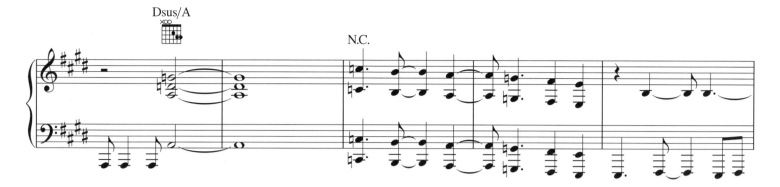

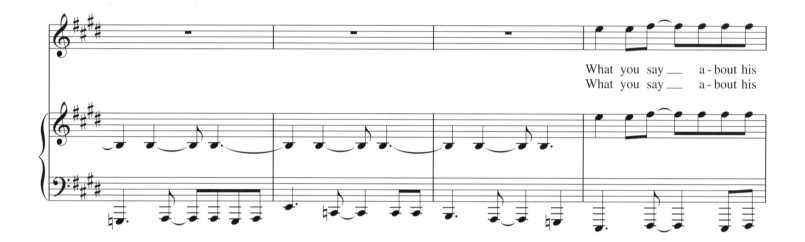

What you say __ a-bout his
What you say __ a-bout his

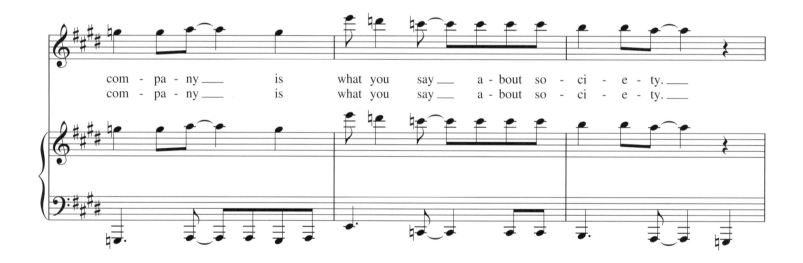

com - pa - ny __ is what you say __ a-bout so - ci - e - ty. __
com - pa - ny __ is what you say __ a-bout so - ci - e - ty. __

Catch the mist, __ catch the myth, __ catch the mys - t'ry,
Catch the wit - ness, catch the wit, __ catch the spir - it,

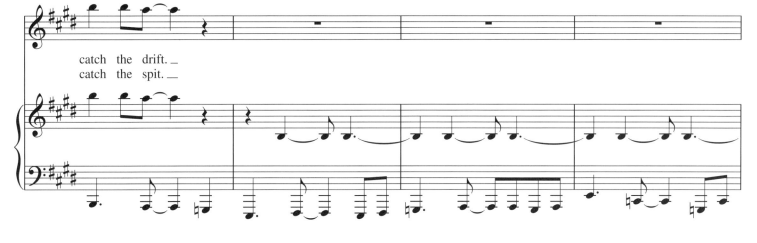

catch the drift. __
catch the spit. __

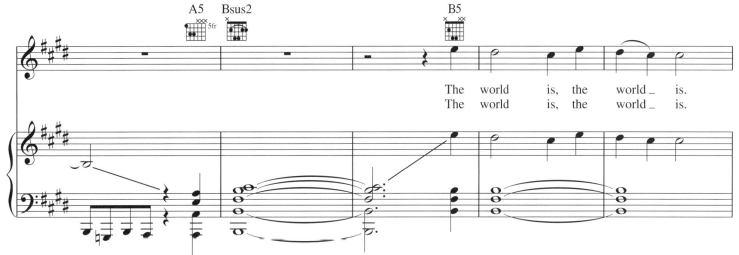

A5 Bsus2   B5

The world   is,   the   world __ is.
The world   is,   the   world __ is.

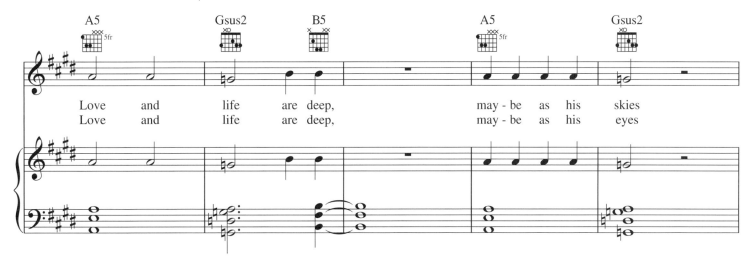

A5   Gsus2   B5   A5   Gsus2

Love   and   life   are deep,   may-be   as   his   skies
Love   and   life   are deep,   may-be   as   his   eyes

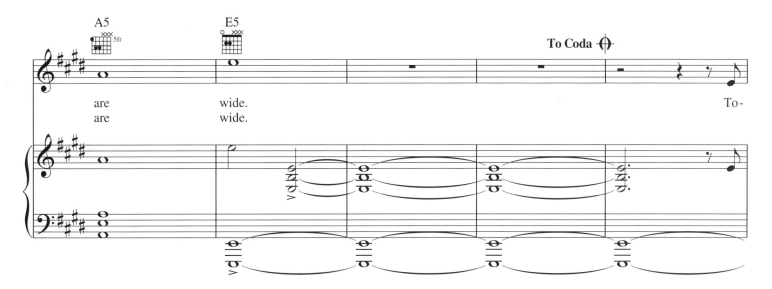

A5   E5   **To Coda** ⊕

are   wide.   To-
are   wide.

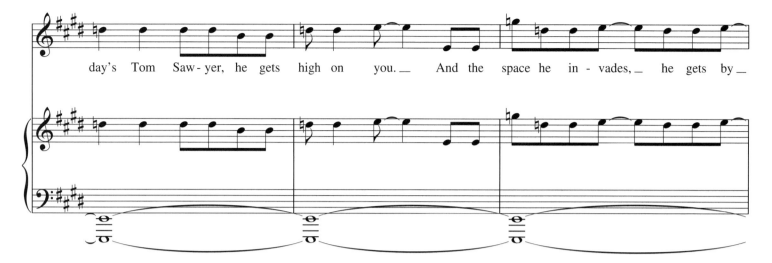

day's Tom Saw- yer, he gets high on you._ And the space he in - vades,_ he gets by_

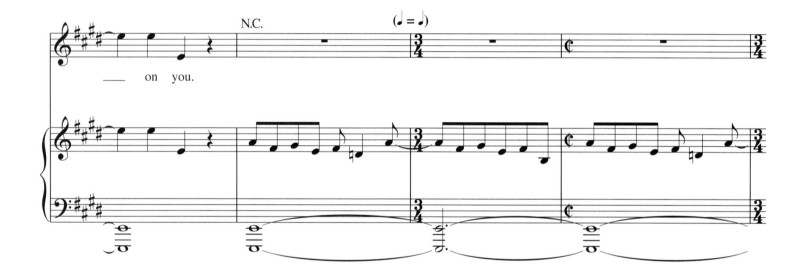

_ on you.

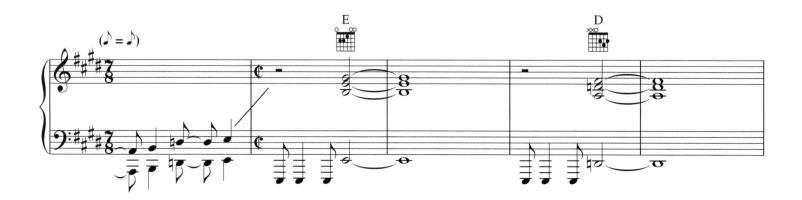

Ex - it the war - ri - or. To - day's Tom Saw - yer, he gets high on you.___ And the

en - er - gy you___ trade he gets right on to the fric - tion of___ the

day.

YOU NEEDED ME

Words and Music by
RANDY GOODRUM

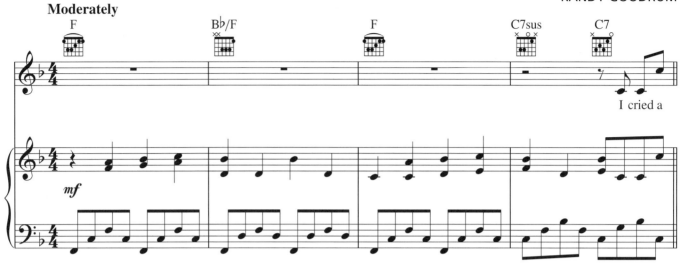

Lyrics:

I cried a tear, you wiped it dry; I was con-fused, you cleared my mind. I sold my soul, you bought it back for me __ and held me

hand when it was cold; when I was lost, you took me home. You gave me hope when I was at the end __ and turned my

© 1975 (Renewed) CHAPPELL & CO., INC. and IRONSIDE MUSIC
All Rights Administered by CHAPPELL & CO., INC.
All Rights Reserved   Used by Permission

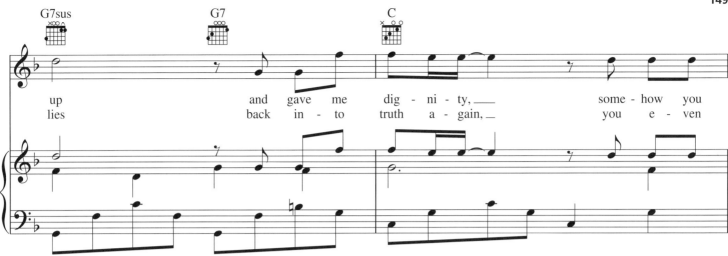

up ___ and gave me dig - ni - ty, ___ some - how you
lies ___ back in - to truth a - gain, ___ you e - ven

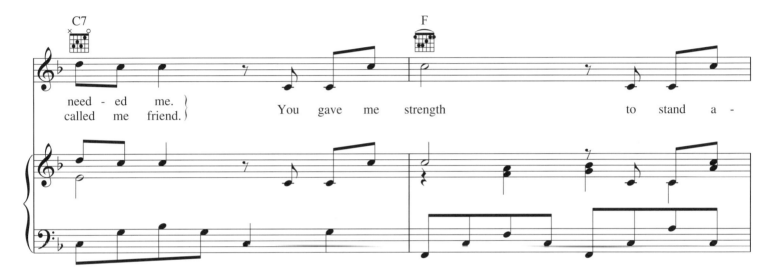

need - ed me. }
called me friend. } You gave me strength to stand a -

lone a - gain, ___ to face the world, out on my

own a - gain. ___ You put me high up - on a

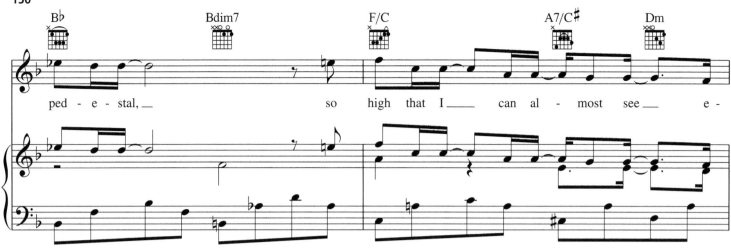

ped - e - stal, ___ so high that I ___ can al - most see ___ e -

ter - ni - ty. ___ You need - ed me, ___ you

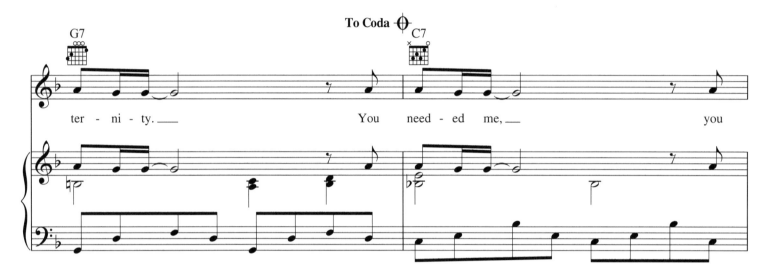

need - ed me. ___ And I can't be - lieve it's you, ___ I can't be - lieve ___

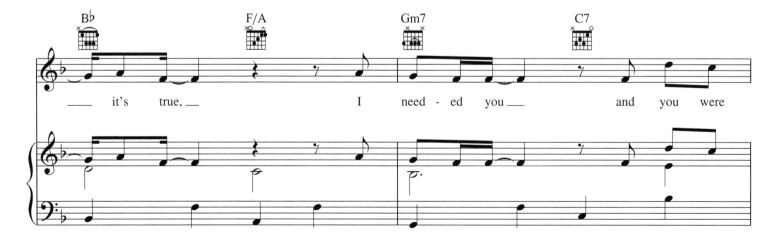

___ it's true, ___ I need - ed you ___ and you were

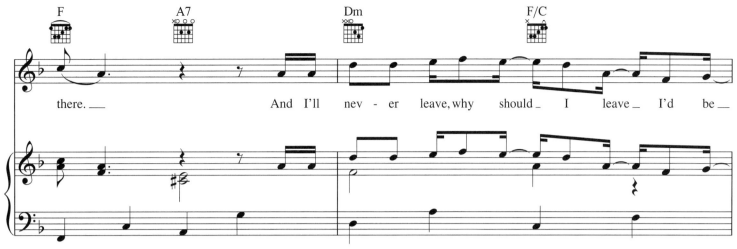

there. ___ And I'll nev - er leave, why should ___ I leave ___ I'd be ___

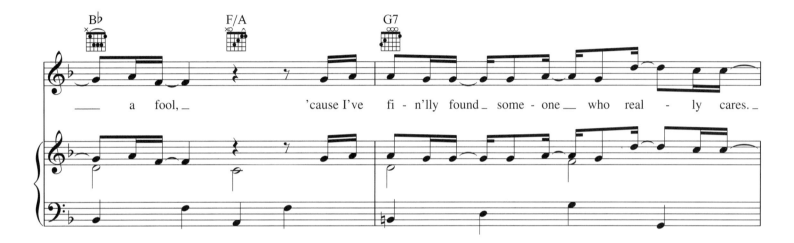

___ a fool, ___ 'cause I've fi - n'lly found ___ some - one ___ who real - ly cares. ___

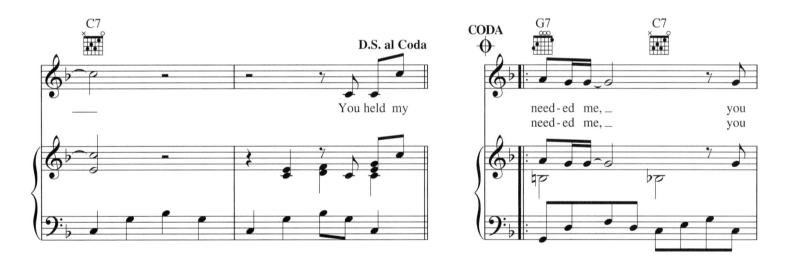

D.S. al Coda

___ You held my

CODA

need - ed me, ___ you
need - ed me, ___ you

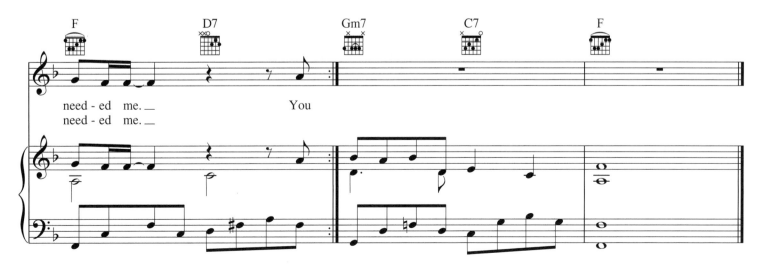

need - ed me. ___ You
need - ed me. ___

YOU'RE STILL THE ONE

Words and Music by SHANIA TWAIN
and R.J. LANGE

Copyright © 1997 LOON ECHO, INC. and OUT OF POCKET PRODUCTIONS, LTD.
All Rights for LOON ECHO, INC. Controlled and Administered by SONGS OF UNIVERSAL, INC.
All Rights for OUT OF POCKET PRODUCTIONS, LTD. in the U.S. and Canada Administered by UNIVERSAL - POLYGRAM INTERNATIONAL PUBLISHING, INC.
All Rights Reserved   Used by Permission

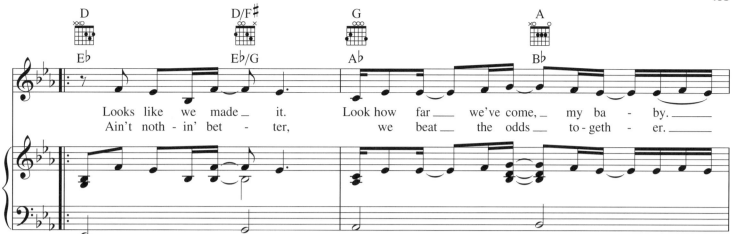

Looks like we made it. Look how far we've come, my ba by.
Ain't noth-in' bet ter, we beat the odds to-geth er.

We might-a took the long way. We knew we'd get there some day.
I'm glad we did-n't lis ten. Look at what we would be miss ing.

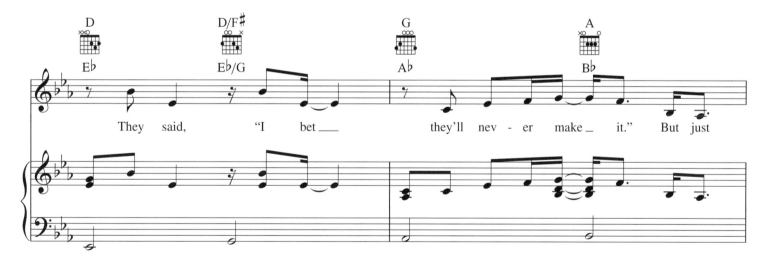

They said, "I bet they'll nev-er make it." But just

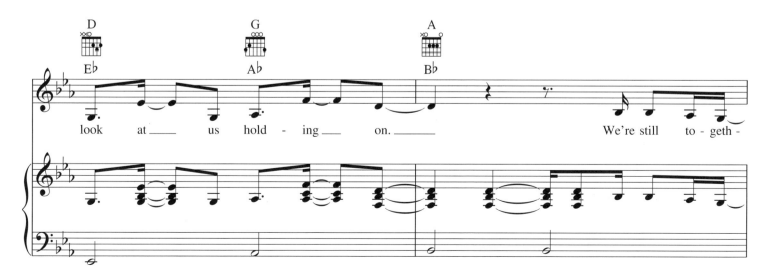

look at us hold-ing on. We're still to-geth-

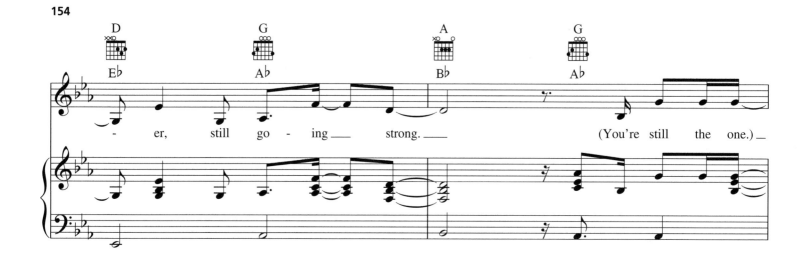

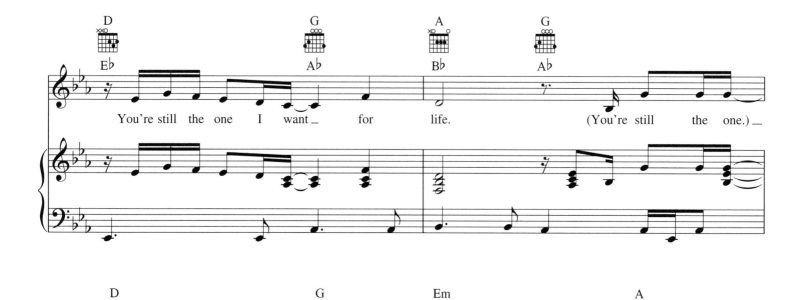

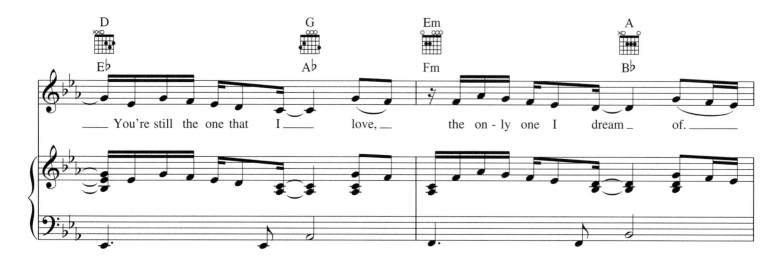

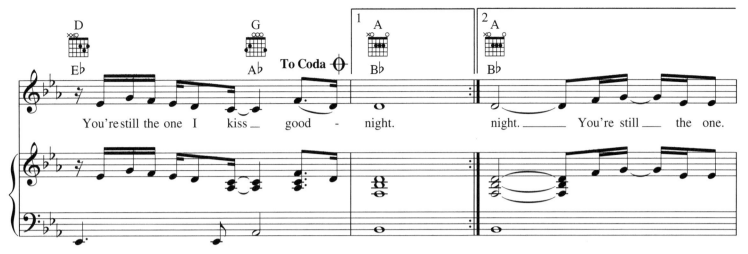

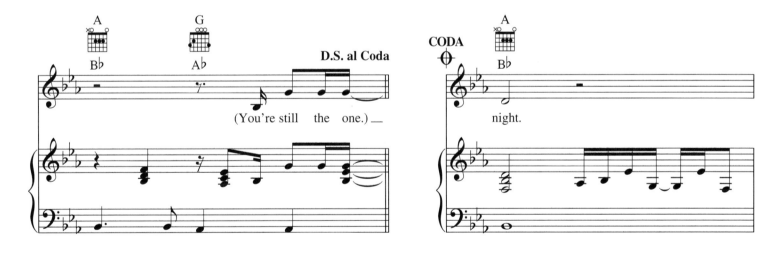

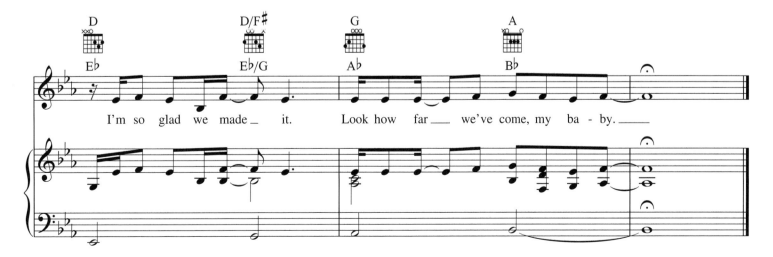

YOU LEARN

Lyrics by ALANIS MORISSETTE
Music by ALANIS MORISSETTE and GLEN BALLARD

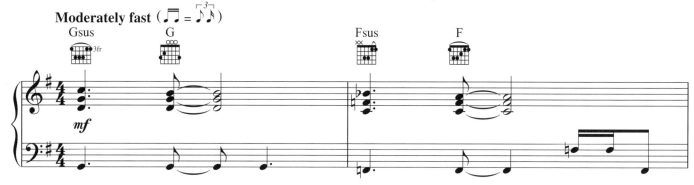

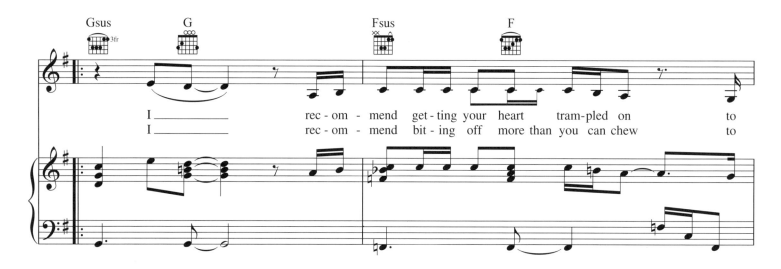

I _____ rec-om-mend get-ting your heart tram-pled on to
I _____ rec-om-mend bit-ing off more than you can chew to

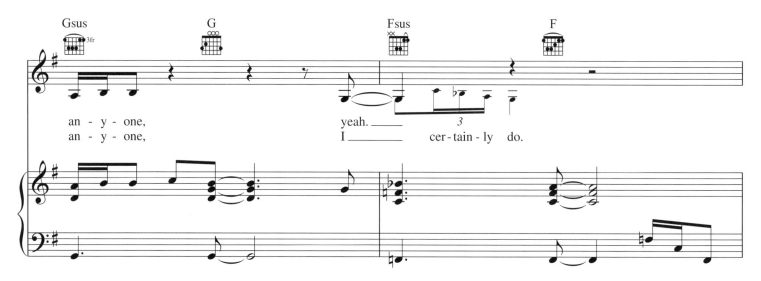

an-y-one, yeah. _____ I _____ cer-tain-ly do.
an-y-one,

Copyright © 1995 SONGS OF UNIVERSAL, INC., VANHURST PLACE, UNIVERSAL MUSIC CORP. and AEROSTATION CORPORATION
All Rights for VANHURST PLACE Controlled and Administered by SONGS OF UNIVERSAL, INC.
All Rights for AEROSTATION CORPORATION Controlled and Administered by UNIVERSAL MUSIC CORP.
All Rights Reserved   Used by Permission

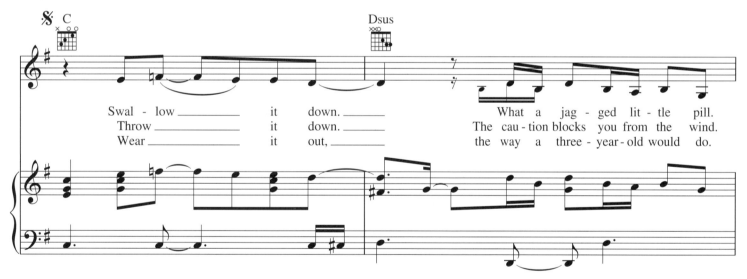

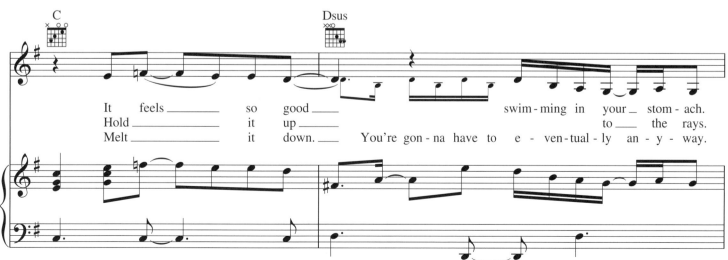

Wait un - til _____ the dust set
You wait _____ and _____ see when _ the smoke _____ clears. _____
The fire - trucks _ are _____ com-ing up a - round the bend. _

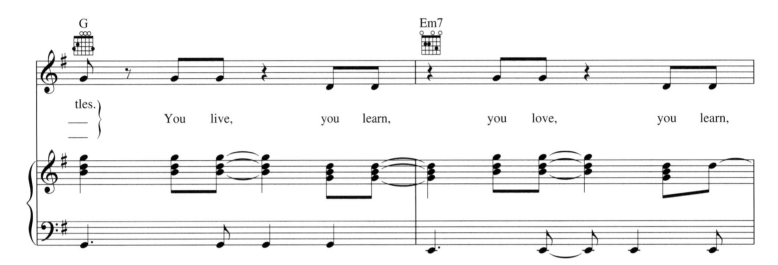

tles.)
You live, you learn, you love, you learn,

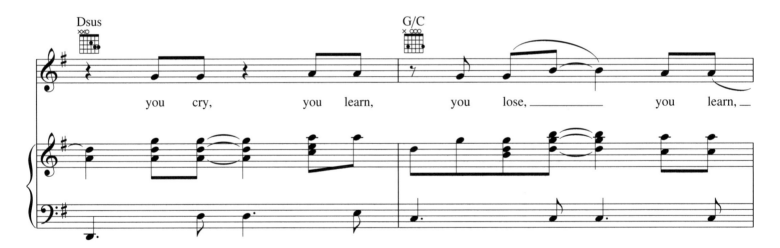

you cry, you learn, you lose, _____ you learn, _

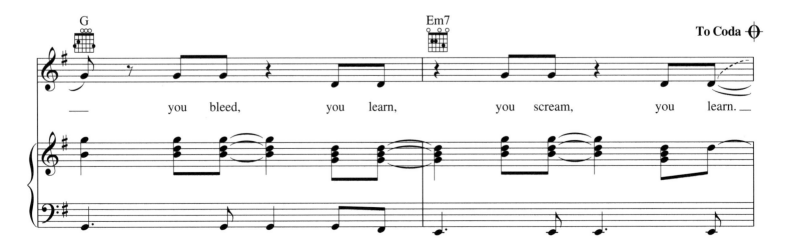

you bleed, you learn, you scream, you learn. _

To Coda

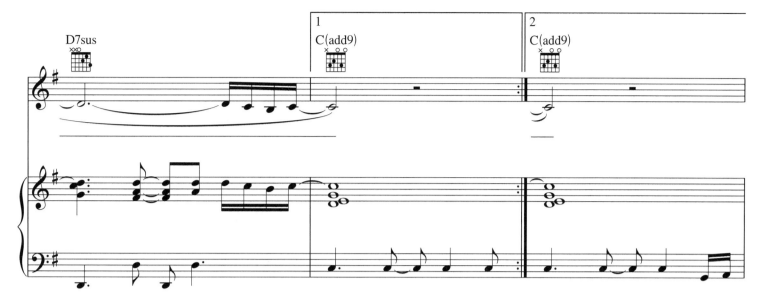

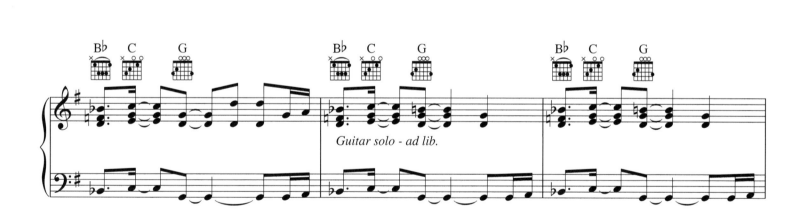

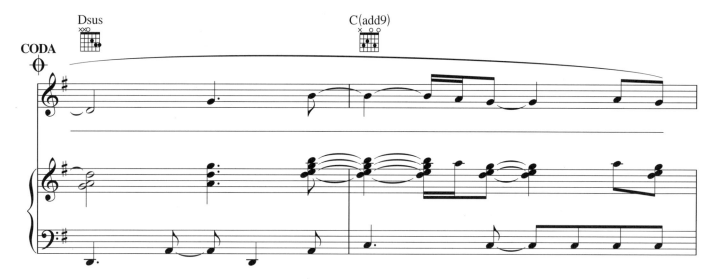

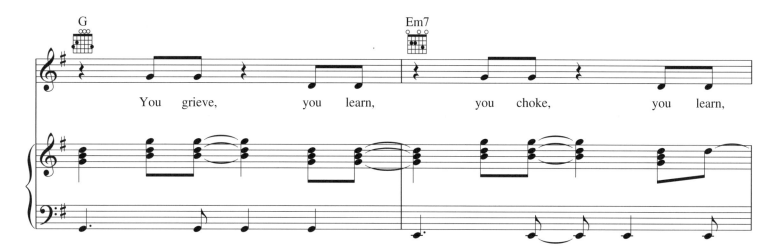

You grieve, you learn, you choke, you learn,

you laugh, you learn, you choose, ___ you learn, ___ you pray, you learn,

you ask, you learn, you live, you learn. ___